화쟁(和諍) 그리기: 상상을 위한 분쟁지역 매핑

Drawing Hwa-Chaeng: Mapping Contested Territories for Imagi-nation

김동세
Dongsei Kim

"Is that a snake?" My two-year-old son asked, looking at the long and slender black line on my computer screen. Perhaps my mapping of the Korean Demilitarized Zone was successful enough to activate my son's imagination and spark a conversation. In many ways, my mapping projects are about revealing the possibilities of a place and setting in motion multiple imaginations.

Moreover, mapping is one of several process-driven methods I deploy in my creative practice that aim to critique and better understand a generic 'space' as a meaningful 'place.' I trust that this approach offers a productive platform where better futures for the existing can emerge. Mapping is an essential and fundamental part of how I research and practice.

I believe a good mapping project leads you to generate conditions for multiple meaningful questions to materialize rather than merely providing a solution to a predetermined question. Mapping is an opening-up tool for exploring possibilities rather than finding a solution for my practice.

"저거 뱀이야?" 두 살배기 아들이 내 컴퓨터 화면에 비친 '길고 가느다란 검은 선'을 바라보며 물었다. 아마도 나의 비무장지대 매핑은 이 아이의 상상력을 자극하고 대화를 유발할 만큼 성공적이었나 보다. 이처럼 나의 매핑 프로젝트들은 어떠한 장소의 가능성을 드러내며 여러 상상력을 활성화시키는 것이다.

나의 매핑은 나의 창작 활동에서 행해지는 여러 과정 중심 방법 중 하나이다. 나는 이 접근 방식이 현재보다 더 나은 미래를 불러올 수 있는 생산적인 플랫폼을 제공한다고 믿고 있다. 매핑은 나의 연구와 실무 과정에 필수적이고 근본적인 요소이다. 좋은 매핑은 미리 정해진 질문에 대한 해법을 단순히 제공하기보다는 여러 개의 의미 있는 질문이 구체화될 수 있는 여건을 조성한다. 그런 점에서 매핑은 나에게 해결책을 찾기보다는 가능성을 탐색하게끔 하는 개방적 도구이다.

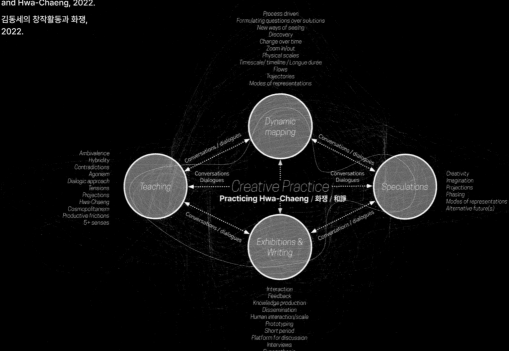

My mapping projects engage an expansive range of physical scales and timescales that provide a wide range of perspectives and a long-term point of view for the selected site and its related issues. They aim to generate new ways of understanding and seeing a place; cumulatively, they become new knowledge and critical ingredients for design. Each of my mapping projects is interconnected to each other through stories and iterations of the past. They narrate and challenge the status quo through subversive approaches that are projective and imaginative, which start to test the limitations of mapping practices.

Parts of why I map, how I map, and what I map are documented in this publication. It offers a glimpse into my research practice and how I use mapping as a process to open up possibilities and as a method to meaningfully expand architectural practices. In the following section, I expand on how I consider my mapping projects to be a form of performing Hwa-Chaeng that provokes and sparks conversations between opposing parties.

나의 매핑은 광범위한 물리적, 시간적 스케일들을 다루며, 연구 대상인 대지와, 그와 관련된 쟁점들에 관한 넓은 시각과 장기적인 관점을 제공한다. 또한 일반적인 '공간'을 의미 있는 '장소'로 새롭게 이해하고, 보는 방법을 제안하는 것을 목표로 한다. 이러한 과정이 쌓이면 새로운 지식과 중요한 디자인 요소가 더욱 풍부해진다. 궁극적으로는 현재를 설명하고 현실에 도전하며 관행적인 기존 매핑의 한계를 시험한다.

이 책에서는 내가 매핑하는 이유와 방법 그리고 대상과 내용에 관해 이야기하고자 한다. 아울러 새로운 가능성을 열어주는 과정으로서 매핑, 건축 실무를 의미 있게 확장시키는 방법으로서 매핑을 나의 연구 프로젝트를 통해 보여줄 것이다. 곧 대립하는 주체들 간의 대화를 유발하는 화쟁(和諍)의 한 형태로 전개될 것이다.

Tiki-taka and Hwa-Chaeng: Conversations and Asking Meaningful Questions

티키타카와 화쟁: 대화와 의미 있는 질문하기

Tiki-Taka refers to a Spanish football playing style characterized by short passing and movement, working the ball through various channels, and maintaining possession. In our case, it is used to describe the act of passing ideas off one another in an informal way to test and further refine emerging ideas and thoughts through a series of conversations and dialogues. And most importantly, to collaborate and support each other's work.

Tiki-Taka's collaborators were located in three different countries and time zones. New York (EST, UTC-5), Hawaii (HST, UTC-10), and Seoul (KST, UTC+9). Current pandemic conditions have made online collaborations like this more common. They effectively minimize geographical distances between people and connect collectives and individuals with similar interests around the globe; at the same time, they distort our spatio-temporal experiences.

My sketch of 'Tiki-Taka' (page 7) on the right illustrates the unique collaborative space within the shrunk world that allowed our productive conversations. So, what does the speed of the internet connection mean to the changing ways architects and designers research, practice, and collaborate? This is one of the many compelling questions we generated through our Tiki-Taka

티키타카는 짧은 패스와 움직임, 다양한 기술로 높은 공 점유율을 유지하는 것이 특징인 스페인의 축구 전술을 말한다. 우리의 경우, 일련의 대화를 통해 떠오르는 아이디어와 생각을 시험하고 다듬기 위해 서로 아이디어를 격식 없이 전달하는 행위를 설명할 때, 티키타카라는 용어를 사용한다. 그리고 이 과정에서 가장 중요한 것은 서로 협력하고 격려하는 것이었다.

티키타카의 협력자들은 세 개의 다른 시간대에 있는 뉴욕(EST, UTC-5), 하와이(HST, UTC-10), 서울(KST, UTC+9)에 위치하고 있었다. 현재의 코로나 팬데믹으로 전 세계의 비슷한 관심사를 가진 집단들과 개인들을 효과적으로 연결해 주는 온라인 협업이 더욱 흔해졌다. 이러한 행위들은 우리의 지리적 거리를 축소함과 동시에 우리의 시공간적 경험을 왜곡시킨다.

다음 페이지에 있는 나의 티키타카 스케치(7쪽)는 우리의 생산적인 대화를 가능하게 하는, 축소된 세계 속의 독특한 협력 공간을 보여준다. 그렇다면, 인터넷의 속도는 건축가와 디자이너가 연구하고, 실무하고, 협력하는 방식에 무슨 의미가 있을까? 이것은 우리의 티키타카 대화 속에서 제기된 질문들 중 하나이다. 또한, 이러한 집단적 경험은 새로운 지식을 함께 창출하는 또 다른 방법을 고찰하기에

Drawing Hwa-Chaeng

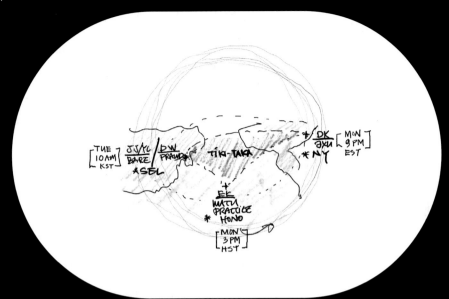

conversations. Further, this collective experience engendered thought-provoking questions about new ways of generating new knowledge together. This publication is a partial documentation of this 20-month collective experience.

"Drawing Hwa-Chaeng: Mapping Contested Territories for Imagination" is the title of my publication. "Drawing Hwa-Chaeng" engages my research on the Korean Demilitarized Zone (DMZ) to illustrate how "Hwa-Chaeng" informed mapping can produce new knowledge that can reframe contentious territories as synergistic productive spaces. This study explicitly engages the "Hwa-Chaeng" philosophy that argues for embracing 'opponents' and working towards reconciliation through continuous conversations. This approach seeks to shift antagonisms beyond false dichotomies and binary oppositions.

Hwa-Chaeng is a philosophy and a working method that Won Hyo (617 - 686) — who was one of the leading thinkers, writers, and commentators of the Korean Buddhist tradition — established when he attempted to address and reconcile contradictory Buddhist sectarianism in the 7th century. According to Hokün Chön, a Korean philosopher, in his book the "History of Korean Philosophy" states that:

이르렀다. 책은 약 20개월에 걸친 집단적 경험과 대화를 기록한 일부이다

《화쟁 그리기: 상상을 위한 분쟁지역 매핑》이라는 제목대로 한반도 비무장지대라는 분쟁지역을 대상으로 한 매핑 프로젝트를 설명한다. 나의 비무장지대 매핑은 '상대'에 대한 포용과 화해를 위해 노력하자는 '화쟁' 사상을 명시적으로 담고 있으며, 접근법에서는 기존의 잘못된 '이원적 대립'이 생산하는 '적대적 지역'을 생산적이며 시너지적인 공간으로 새롭게 정의하고자 한다.

화쟁(和諍)은 7세기 초 한국 불교계의 대표적 승려, 사상가, 작가, 해설가 중 한 명인 원효(617-686)가 모순된 불교 종파주의를 고찰하고 해소하고자 확립한 철학적 접근법이자 작업 방식이다. 한국철학자 전호근은 그의 저서 《한국 철학사》에서 화쟁에 대해 다음과 같이 기술하고 있다:

먼저, '화(和)'는 화합, 통합의 논리입니다. '쟁(諍)'은 '말씀 언(言)'에 '다툴 쟁(爭)'으로 이루어져 있으니까 말로 다투는 것, 싸움입니다. 이렇게 보면 화쟁론은 온갖 '쟁(諍)'을 화해시키는 논리, 곧 '쟁(諍)'을 '화(和)'한다는 논리입니다. 그런가 하면 화쟁의 '화(和)'와 '쟁(諍)' 자체가 상반되는 뜻이죠. 그래서 '화'와 '쟁' 자체는 대립되지만 '화'와 '쟁'이 다른 것이 아니라 모두 진리를 찾기 위한 방편이라는 논리에 도달하는 것이 화쟁론의 특징이기도 합니다(전호근 2015, 24-25).[1]

화쟁(和諍) 그리기

First, the 'Hwa (和)' character of "Hwa-Chaeng" is the logic of concord and consolidation. The second character, 'Chaeng (諍)' is made up of 'speaking ŏn (言)' and 'argument chaeng (爭)', which is about arguing and debating through words. Therefore, the theory of Hwa-Chaeng is about reconciling all kinds of chaeng (諍), thus reconciling 'chaeng (諍) arguments' into a form of 'Hwa (和) consolidation' through conversations and arguments. At the same time, Hwa-Chaeng's Hwa (和) and Chaeng (諍) may be understood as the opposite to each other. The defining character of the Hwa-Chaeng theory is arriving at the understanding that this seemingly opposite Hwa and Chaeng are not different from each other but understanding both as different ways of seeking the truth (Chŏn 2015, 24-25)[1].

Hwa-Chaeng was one of the many approaches and philosophies I encountered and embraced in my decade-long research on nation-state borders. For example, Richard Sennett's dialogical[2] approach, which favors exchanges of ideas in an open-ended framework over producing a definitive resolution, and Chantal Mouffe's agonistic[3] approach, which favors confronting different perspectives without the possibility of reconciling them into

'화쟁'은 내가 지난 10년 동안 한반도 분단 상황과 국경에 대해 연구하면서 받아들인 많은 접근법과 철학 논리 중 하나다. 유사하게는 리처드 세넷의 대화적(dialogic)[2] 접근은 완결된 해결책을 도출하는 것보다 개방형 프레임워크 안에서 아이디어를 교환하도록 하고, 샹탈 무페의 대립적 (아고니즘적)[3] 접근방식은 여러 갈등을 하나의 숙고된 형태로 조화시킬 가능성을 배제하고 다양한 시각과 관점에 직면하도록 권한다.[4]

나는 티키타카의 대화에서 한반도 분쟁의 이슈를 다룰 때도 화쟁을 발현시키는 방법이 적절하다고 확신한다.

궁극적으로는 이 출판물이 매핑에 대한 나의 접근법이자, 화쟁을 실천하는 방법이다. 나의 독특한 세계관이기도 한 '코즈모폴리턴'으로서의 정체성에서부터 공간적으로 표출되는 현상까지, 다양한 스케일로 매핑한 프로젝트들이 담겨 있다. 매핑 프로젝트들은 다분히 논쟁적인 경계/국경에 대한 여러 관점을 제공할 뿐만 아니라, 논쟁/분쟁에 대한 대안적 가능성을 촉발한다. 단절/분단이 야기하는 정체성/민족국가, 경계/국경의 특성에 의문을 제기하고, 비무장지대(DMZ)에 대한 지배적 인식에 도전한다. 또한 국가의 경계선들이 디아스포라와 이산가족들의 일상에 어떠한 영향을 미치는지에 대한 질문을 던지며 이에 관한 대화들을 제안한다.

Drawing Hwa-Chaeng

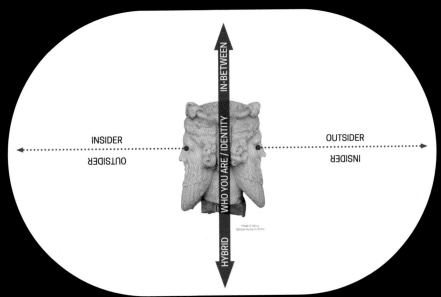

one deliberated form are some of the conceptual
frameworks that my work on the Korean division
and borders are founded upon.[4]

I am convinced that engaging the Korean
Buddhist scholar Won Hyo's Hwa-Chaeng through
the lens of mapping to address the Korean conflict
within this Tiki-Taka conversation is an appropriate
way to examine the agency of mapping that
engender new imaginaries for contested territories.

The publication aims to articulate how my
approach to mapping as a method enables the
practicing of Hwa-Chaeng. It starts with a spread
that maps my cosmopolitan identity that informs my
particular way of seeing the world. The book then
introduces a series of mapping projects at various
scales that represent the existing conditions
through spatial means. These primary research
mapping projects generate ingredients for multiple
points of view of the contested border, instigating
alternative possibilities for the contested territory.

These mapping projects further challenge
the dominant representations of the Demilitarized
Zone (DMZ) that raise questions and instigate
dialogues about the nation-state, the nature of its
borders, and how they impact the daily lives of the
separated families and diasporas.

1.
Chön, Hokŭn. 2015. 『Han-kuk
ch'ŏl-hak-sa (한국 철학사/History
of Korean Philosophy)』 Seoul:
Memento. [Original text in
Korean, translated by Dongsei
Kim. pp. 24-25.

2.
Sennett, Richard. 2012.
『Together: The Rituals, Pleasures
and Politics of Cooperation』 New
Haven: Yale University Press. pp.
18-19.

3.
Mouffe, Chantal 2008. "Agonistic
Public Spaces: Democratic
Politics and the Dynamics of
Passions" in 『Thinking Worlds
: The Moscow Conference on
Philosophy, Politics, and Art』
edited by Joseph Backstein,
Daniel Birnbaum,and Sven-Olov
Wallenstein. Berlin ; New York,
NY : Moscow: Sternberg Press.
pg. 101.

4.
Also see: Kim, Dongsei. 2014.
"Towards a Dialogical Peace
in the Demilitarized Zone."
『Volume』 40 (July): 40-43.

Conversation with Luaks Pauer: Efficacy & Pitfalls of Mapping

루카스 파우어와의 대화: 매핑의 효력과 함정

This text is an excerpt from one of the ongoing conversations with my colleague Lukas Pauer. This two-hour-long conversation was held on Zoom in August 2021. It focused on the role of mapping in architectural research. Further, it explored why and how I deploy mapping in my creative practice, especially as a tool to address conflicts that are spatial in nature. This conversation starts with the discussion of my "The Second Iteration: Uncovering the Agency of the Unknown Armistice Maps"(pages 50-53) exhibition in 2017. The short excerpt of the conversation was edited for clarity.

이 글은 나의 동료인 루카스 파우어와의 대화에서 일부를 발췌한 것이다. 2021년 8월 줌 미팅을 통해 두 시간여 이루어진 대화는 건축 연구에서 매핑의 역할에 초점을 맞추었다. 특히 본질적으로 공간적인 갈등을 다루는 도구로서 매핑을 내가 왜, 그리고 어떻게 사용하는지를 논의했다. 여기서는 매핑의 효용성과 한계를 다루되, 나의 작업 가운데 하나인 "두 번째 반복: 알려지지 않은 정전협정 지도의 힘/역할 발굴하기, 2017"(50~53쪽) 전시로 얘기를 시작한다. 해당 대화는 명확성을 위해 편집되었다.

Dongsei Kim (DK): Mapping from the exhibition "The Second Iteration" in 2017 (pages 50-53) attempts to engage the non-visual communication such as other sensory experiences that complement the typically visually dominant ways of communicating. This exhibition includes interrogation of the relationship between the 'line drawn on a map' and the disjunctive spatial result produced over time. It also introduced non-visual senses that complement typical maps that are typically dominated by the visual elements.

Lukas Pauer (LP): Can you say that again differently? The non-visual. What did you mean by that?

DK: So, some of the previous maps that I produced like this, for example (The Second Iteration: Uncovering the Agency of the Unknown Armistice Maps, 2017), were basically moving images (animation) but still visual. However, it started to introduce sound, let's say, how a drawing, or a picture that adds to understanging an atmosphere and experience of a place, further, this approach encourages interaction with the map, especially in the context of an exhibition.

What I was more interested in the following exhibitions was to do something beyond the visual. And because it was an installation within an exhibition space, what I tried to do was to bring in other senses, other than, let's say, the eyes. And the most obvious easy one was to bring in the sound. So, some of the sounds that were documented from the visits that I made to the DMZ were brought into the dynamic video mapping. These colllected sounds were played in a physical exhibition space that complemented these visual materials.

김동세(김): 2017년 작업 "두 번째 반복: 알려지지 않은 정전협정 지도의 힘/역할 발굴하기"(50~53쪽)은 다른 감각적 경험들이 공존한다는 점을 보여주려 한 것인데, 시각 중심의 커뮤니케이션을 보완하는 비시각적 커뮤니케이션 방식을 말하고 싶었다. 이것은 당신이 이미 본 적이 있을 또 다른 매핑인데, 이 매핑은 다른 감각적 경험들이 공존하는 전시라는 맥락에서 이해될 필요가 있다. 여기서 나는 일반적인 시각 중심 커뮤니케이션 방식을 보완하는 비시각적 커뮤니케이션에 대한 이야기한다. "두 번째 반복"은 잘 알려지지 않은 정전협정 지도들을 해체하고 재구성하여 새롭게 해석하는 작업이 포함된 전시였다. 이 전시는 '지도에 그려진 선들'과 시간이 지나면서 생겨난 물리적 공간들 사이의 괴리를 질문했다. 또한 흔히 시각적 감각에 치우친 지도의 특성을 보완하는 비시각적 감각들을 도입했다.

루카스 파우어(파): 비시각적이라... 좀 다르게 말하면 무엇인가?

김: 부연 설명을 하자면, 이전까지 나의 매핑 프로젝트 중 일부는 기본적으로 움직이는 이미지, 즉 애니메이션이지만 여전히 시각적이었다. 하지만 이 작업에서는 드로잉에 소리를 입히기 시작했는데, 매핑이 목표로 하는 소통과 경험을 더해준다. 특히 전시 환경에서는 더더욱 말이다.

그다음 전시에서는 시각적인 것을 초월하는 데 더욱 관심을 가졌다. 내 작업이 한정된 공간 안에서 보여주는 설치물이었기 때문에, 이를테면 전시공간에다 시각 외에 다른 감각들을 불러들이고자 한 것이다. 가장 쉬운 것이 소리를 가져오는 것이었고, 비무장지대를 방문했을 때 채집했던 일부 소리를 동적인 매핑 영상 작업물에 삽입해 보았다. 그리고 전시공간에서 시각적 요소들이 전달하지 못한 부분을 대신해 소리를 틀었다.

Lukas Pauer
University of Toronto / Vertical Geopolitics Lab

Dongsei Kim
New York Institute of Technology / aux studio

So, I started to engage notions of synesthesia often discussed by Maurice Merleau-Ponty[1] that inform the conflation of visual and other senses. Synesthesia and the notion of multiple sensory interactions... you have the hearing, the touching, and all these other senses that start to contribute to a certain kind of experience. So, that that's the point of this particular mapping (The Second Iteration, 2017). The drawing is important, but other elements are important too.

For example, some of these texts - here are sometimes keywords, sometimes they are words that mimic sounds, like "tick-tock tick-tock..." that is about the flow of time. These words were also projected on the wall. It was a kind of a mixed media work that was beyond just the screen itself. It was an attempt to bring materials and contents of the mapping out from the screen, to encourage more interaction with the audience beyond the visual that would provoke their visceral experience. Here I am using mapping as a tool, a mediator to, let's say, facilitate and direct certain kinds of conversations and stimulate questions, rather than to provide, you know, predetermined knowledge or solution.

나는 모리스 메를로퐁티[1]가 자주 언급한 공감각 (synesthesia)에도 계속 관심을 갖고 있다. 공감각과 다중감각의 상호작용 말이다. 청각, 촉각, 그 밖의 다른 감각들이 모여 어떠한 특정 경험을 만들어낸다. 바로 이것이 2017년 드로잉 전시의 요점이다. 드로잉 그 자체도 중요하지만, 그 외의 다른 요소들도 아주 중요하다.

예를 들자면, 키워드 중에는 소리를 흉내 내는 단어들이 있다. 시간의 흐름을 표현하는 '똑딱 똑딱' 같은 말들이다. 이러한 단어들이 전시장 벽에 비추어졌다. 영상이 재생되는 스크린을 넘어서는 일종의 혼합 미디어 작품이었다. 이는 매핑의 재료와 내용을 화면 밖으로 끄집어내려는 시도였고, 관람객의 본능적인 경험을 자극해 시각에만 의존하는 소통 보다 훨씬 더 많은 상호작용을 꾀하는 것이었다. 여기서 나는 매핑을 중재적 도구로 사용한다. 미리 결정된 지식이나 해결책을 제시하는 것이 아닌, 어떤 특정한 대화를 도모하고 여러 질문을 던지도록 하는 도구이다.

1.
Merleau-Ponty, Maurice. 1962. 『Phenomenology of Perception』 Trans., Colin Smith, London: Routledge and Kegan Paul.

화쟁(和諍) 그리기

P: So, I think I would like to tease out what you said a little earlier about that project ("The Second Iteration," 2017) where you introduced audio sensations and visual dominance. I am curious as to why you introduced the auditory senses to the visually dominated mapping media and what do you think may be the limitation of mapping?

DK: I think your observation is pretty accurate in the way these other senses are sort of additional layers if you call it that. Adding other senses to the visually dominated map was to compliment some of the limitations of a map that certainly gives priority to what you see as the visual that is dominant in architectural culture, it's visually driven. I don't necessarily see itself as a problem. However, when the visual becomes too dominant, I think it becomes problematic. What I am trying to do is to at least bring attention to the fact that there are other important senses, other than the visual, which contribute to producing one's knowledge and experience.

LP: It might not be an easy one to begin with. But I can see a lot of timelines and borderlines in your work. And since both timelines and borderlines are rooted in a very Euro-Western genealogy way of seeing the world in terms of their epistemology, they are clearly related to certain Euro-Western agencies of power. I am wondering how aware you are in your work and how they are related to each other. I mean, what is your stance in relation to these important issues? Is this something that you were conscious of?

DK: In this context, one of the fundamental questions that I explore through my mapping projects is, "How can we use the tools that one has used to exploit in a subversive way to counter their effects." It may be possible, and I guess that's the kind of exploration that I am having here with my mapping. However, there is always this question of, you know, should you just use a different, a totally different, a completely new tool (that is not mapping) to remedy the problems of Euro-centric system

파: 언급한 프로젝트("두 번째 반복, 2017")에 대해 다른 질문을 해보고 싶다. 지배적인 시각에 청감각을 처음 결합하게 된 이유가 궁금하다. 매핑의 역할에 어떤 한계가 있다고 생각하는가?

김: 감각들이 일종의 다른 층위(層位)에 있다는 점에서 당신의 질문은 꽤나 통찰력 있고 정확하다. 매핑에 시각 이외의 감각을 더하는 일은 매핑의 한계점을 보완하고자 하는 목적이 있다. 건축문화도 마찬가지다. 시각을 우선시하는 것 자체가 문제라고는 생각지 않지만, 시각이 지나치게 강조되고 지배적이면 문제가 된다고 생각한다. 이 점은 지식과 경험에도 해당된다고 보는데, 한 개인이 생산하는 지식과 경험에는 여러 감각이 작용한다. 그 사실에 주목하게 하는 것이 내가 하려는 것이다.

파: 쉽지 않은 질문일 수 있겠다. 당신의 작업에서는 타임라인과 국가 경계선들을 자주 볼 수 있다. 모두 인식론적 관점에서 볼 때, 매우 유럽 중심적이고 서양적 세계관에 뿌리를 두고 있는 것들이다. 특정한 기득권과도 분명히 연관된다. 이들이 서로 어떠한 방식으로 연관되어 있는지, 얼마나 알고 있는가? 다시 말해, 이러한 쟁점에 대한 당신의 입장은 무엇인가? 이미 의식한 부분인가?

김: 그 맥락에서 보자면, 근본적인 질문을 하나 해볼 수 있다. 그 질문은, 어떻게 하면, 역사적으로 권력자들이 자원, 생산 수단, 및 노동력을 착취하는 도구로 사용된 매핑이 전복적인 접근 방식을 통해서 그 착취의 여파를 상쇄시킬 수 있는가이다. 전혀 불가능해 보이지 않는 이 작업이 나에게는 일종의 탐험인 셈이다. 당신도 알다시피, 유럽 중심적인 착취의 시스템을 극복하려면 매핑이 아닌, 전혀 다른, 완전히 새로운 도구가 필요하지 않냐는 회의는 항상 제기된다.

Sample 3D Print of DMZ topography at 1:50,000 scale,
(Using Ultimaker S5, PLA, 3.15 × 3.15″ / 80 × 80 mm), 2021.
DMZ 1:50,000 스케일 지형의 3D 프린트 샘플,
2021.

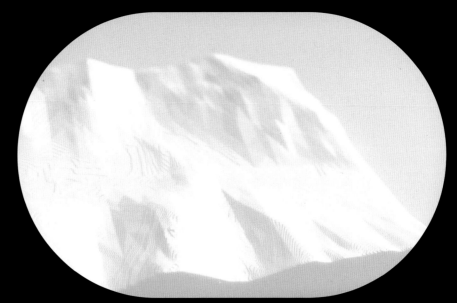

LP: How do you distinguish mapping from design? Part of mapping is design. How is mapping relevant to the discipline of design for you?

DK: That's a good question, and I think mapping for me is a form of design. As mentioned, in the "The Agency of Mapping,"[2] mapping is not just tracing, but it is actually a project in itself that you make, which I see as a design process. So, a good mapping that allows you to, in this case, let's say, determine a program for a site with a very good reasoning and meaning is enough to be categorized as design. In some cases, mapping can become a powerful tool to justify not to build for a certain time and location. Therefore, in many ways, I say that mapping is a form of design.

As another example, what I am interested in doing with my students in the DMZ studios I teach is having the students map the border territory with some given ingredients so that they can specify their own site, which, you know, the mapping, in a way, becomes a critical driver for where the site could be with a meaningful program. So as a tool, when I say mapping is productive is when the process can produce meaning for a selected site and programs that generate questions that open up multiple possibilities.

파: 당신은 매핑과 디자인을 어떻게 구분하는가? 매핑의 일부가 디자인이지 않은가. 당신에게 매핑은 디자인으로서 어떤 의의가 있는가?

김: 좋은 질문이다. 매핑은 나에게도 일종의 디자인이다. 《매핑의 힘/역할》[2]에서 언급하듯이, 매핑은 단순히 무엇을 따라 그리는 것이 아니라, 우리가 직접 만드는 그 자체로서 프로젝트이며, 이를 나는 디자인 프로세스라고 본다. 어떤 대지에 대해 논리적이고 유의미한 프로그램을 만들 수 있게끔 하는 매핑은 좋은 매핑이고, 디자인이기에 이미 충분하다. 어떤 경우에는 특정한 시점과 위치에 건물을 짓지 말아야 한다는 것을 정당화하는 강력한 도구가 될 수도 있다. 그래서 나는 매핑을 여러 면에서 디자인의 한 형태라고 간주한다.

또 다른 예를 들면, DMZ를 주제로 스튜디오의 학생들과 작업할 때, 학생들이 여러 정보들을 가지고 국경지대를 매핑하여 각자만의 대지를 선정하도록 한다. 매핑에서 자신이 대지를 직접 선택하는 과정은 중요한 동력이 되기 때문이다. 그래서 내가 매핑을 생산적인 도구라고 얘기할 때는 대지와 그에 알맞은 프로그램에 대해 의미를 만들어 낼 때이다. 또한 가능성을 열어주는 질문을 던질 때이다.

2.
Corner, James. 1999. "The Agency of Mapping: Speculation, Critique and Invention." In 『Mappings』 Edited by Dennis Cosgrove. London: Reaktion Books.

2. Primary school - Dubai, UAE

1. Born - Seoul, Korea

3. Primary & secondary schools - Seoul, Korea

10. Kyunghee University, Suwon, Korea - Adjunct Professor

9. PLAN_C, Seoul, Korea - Architect

18. Korea University, Seoul, Korea - Assistant Professor

14. RMIT University, Melbourne, Australia - Studio Leader

17. University of Melbourne, Melbourne, Australia - PhD candidate

15. Monash University, Melbourne, Australia - Studio Leader

20. RMIT University, Melbourne, Australia - Studio Leader

19. RMIT University, Melbourne, Australia - Studio Leader

4. Secondary school - Wellington, New Zealand

7. Registered Architect (NZRAB) - Wellington, New Zealand

5. Victoria University of Wellington - Wellington, New Zealand - BArch (Hons)

6. CCM Architects - Wellington, New Zealand - Architect

Drawing Hwa-Chaeng

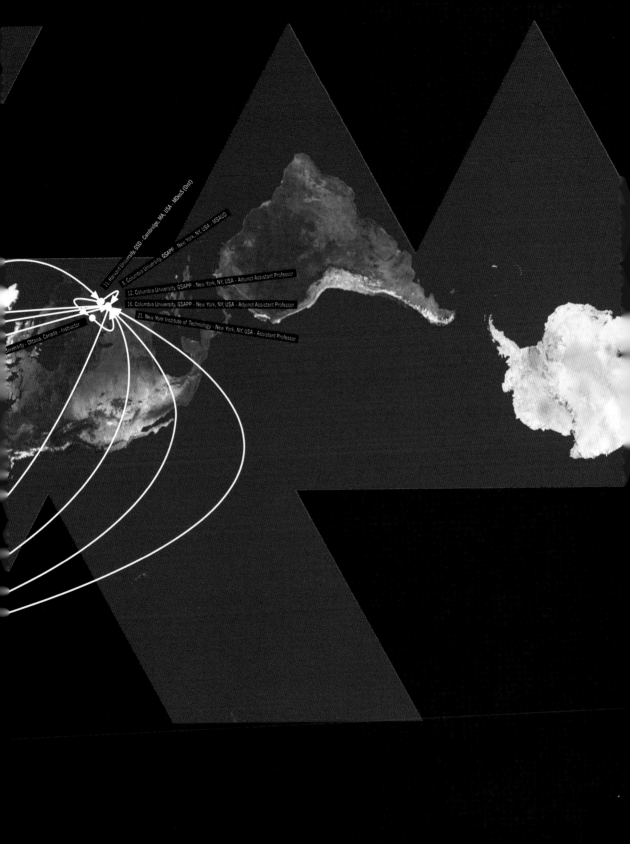

11. Harvard University, GSD - Cambridge, MA, USA - MDesS (Dist)

8. Columbia University, GSAPP - New York, NY, USA - MSAUD

12. Columbia University, GSAPP - New York, NY, USA - Adjunct Assistant Professor

16. Columbia University, GSAPP - New York, NY, USA - Adjunct Assistant Professor

21. New York Institute of Technology - New York, NY, USA - Assistant Professor

University - Ottawa, Canada - Instructor

화쟁(和諍) 그리기

Border Crossing Cosmopolitan Trajectory

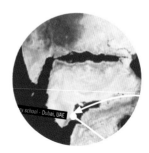

"As architects, we are fascinated by the way things are put together, so the Dymaxion Map also delights the eye and teases the mind. I look at it, and I want to stitch the globe back together again."[1]

"건축가로서 우리는 사물이 조립되는 방식에 매료돼있다. 그러므로 다이맥시온 지도는 우리의 눈을 즐겁게 하고 생각을 자극한다. 나는 지도를 보면 지구를 다시 짜 맞추고 싶다."[1]

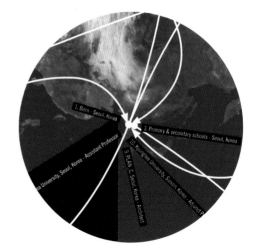

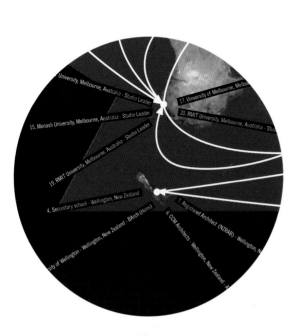

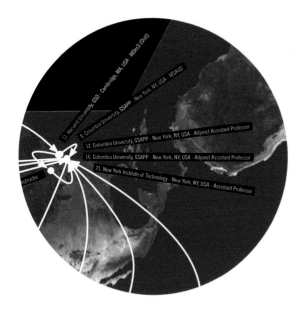

Fuller's Dymaxion Map inspires this mapping.[2] It illustrates my life trajectory and shows a glimpse of how I see and understand the world that impacts how I practice and operate as an architect, urbanist, researcher, and educator.

My border crossing cosmopolitan experience engages many contradictions, hybridities, cosmopolitanism, and ambivalences.

My lived experience and encounters with "others" profoundly impact how I imagine new forms of nation-states through subjective and objective mappings.

이 매핑은 벅민스터 풀러의 다이맥시온 지도에서 영감을 받아 만들어졌다.[2] 이는 내 삶의 이동 경로를 보여줄 뿐만 아니라, 내가 건축가, 도시주의자, 연구자, 교육자로서 활동하는 데 영향을 끼치는 나의 세계관을 엿볼 수 있게끔 한다.

국경을 넘나드는 나의 경험들은 많은 모순성, 혼합성, 세계시민주의(코즈모폴리터니즘), 양면성을 수반한다.

내가 살아온 경험과 '타인'과의 만남은 주관적인 동시에 객관적인 매핑들을 통해, 내가 새로운 형태의 민족국가들을 어떻게 상상하는가에 깊은 영향을 미친다.

NATIONALISM ≠ COSMOPOLITANISM ≠ GLOBALIZATION
국수주의 ≠ 코즈모폴리터니즘 ≠ 세계화

1.
"Deborah Berke on Buckminster Fuller's Dymaxion Map" in 『Metropolis』. https://www.metropolismag.com/ideas/deborah-berke-on-buckminster-fullers-dymaxion-map

2.
Dymaxion Map, Buckminster Fuller (1895-1983)

Dymaxion map embodies Fuller's "dynamic", "maximum," and "tension" approach to design. His map emphasizes connectivity of landmasses by arranging the globe on a developed icosahedron [polyhedron with twenty (icosi) triangular faces and twelve (dodeca) pentagonal faces] planes with minimum distortion. Icosahedron's ability to infinitely reshuffle rejects hierarchy and the "up" or "down" side of a typical. Political borders are eliminated and colored "mean low annual temperature" emphasize ecology and global connectivity.

Tracing the Korean Demilitarized Zone (DMZ)

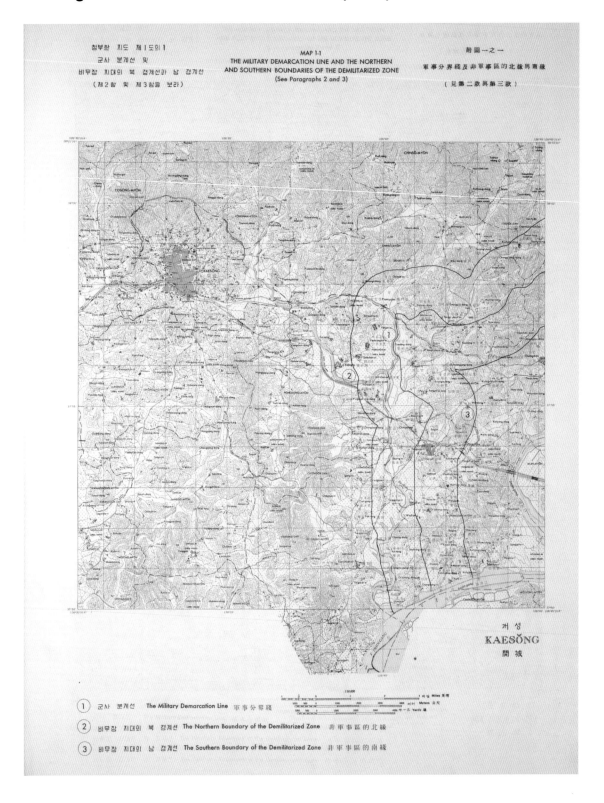

Drawing Hwa-Chaeng

화쟁(和諍) 그리기

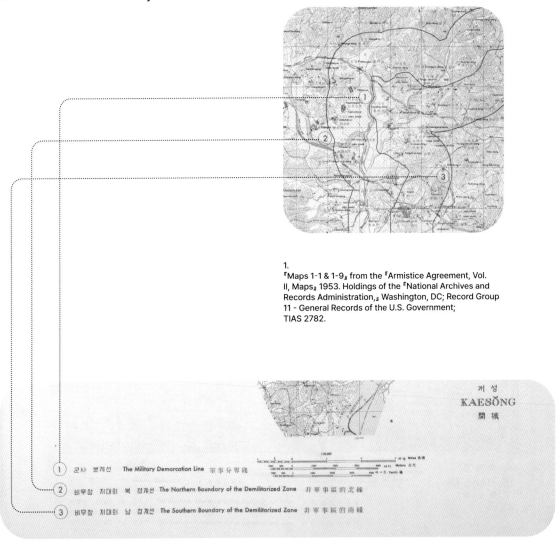

첨부한 지도 제1도의1
군사 분계선 및
비무장 지대의 북 경계선과 남 경계선
(제2항 및 제3항을 보라)

MAP 1-1
THE MILITARY DEMARCATION LINE AND THE NORTHERN
AND SOUTHERN BOUNDARIES OF THE DEMILITARIZED ZONE
(See Paragraphs 2 and 3)

附圖 一之一
軍事分界線及非軍事區的北線與南線
(見第二款與第三款)

"The Armistice Agreement signed on July 27, 1953 and its attached maps are written in Chinese, Korean, and English, and all texts being equally authentic."[1]

 The agreement was signed at Panmunjom at 10:00 hours on July 27, 1953 which took effect at 22:00 hours on the same day.

"1953년 7월 27일 체결된 정전협정과 첨부된 지도는 한글 ("조선 문"), 중국어("중국 문"), 영어("영문") 등 세 가지 언어로 작성되었으며, 각각은 동등한 효력을 가진다."[1]

 이 협정은 1953년 7월 27일 10시에 판문점에서 체결되었고 22시부터 효력이 발생했다.

1.
『Maps 1-1 & 1-9』 from the 『Armistice Agreement, Vol. II, Maps』 1953. Holdings of the 『National Archives and Records Administration,』 Washington, DC; Record Group 11 - General Records of the U.S. Government; TIAS 2782.

거 성
KAESŎNG
開城

① 군사 분계선   The Military Demarcation Line   軍事分界線
② 비무장 지대의 북 경계선   The Northern Boundary of the Demilitarized Zone   非軍事區的北線
③ 비무장 지대의 남 경계선   The Southern Boundary of the Demilitarized Zone   非軍事區的南線

조선 인민군 최고 사령관 및 중국 인민 지원군 사령원을 일방으로 하고 련합국군 총 사령관을 다른 일방으로 하는 조선 군사 정전에 관한 협정

서 언

조선 인민군 최고 사령관 및 중국 인민 지원군 사령원을 일방으로 하고 련합국군 총 사령관을 다른 일방으로 하는 하기의 서명자들은 쌍방에 막대한 고통과 유혈을 초래한 조선 충돌을 정지시키기 위하여서와 최후적인 평화적 해결이 달성될 때까지 조선에서의 적대 행위와 일체 무장 행동의 완전한 정지를 보장하는 정전을 확립할 목적으로 하기 조항에 기재된 정전 조건과 규정을 접수하며 또 그 제약과 통제를 받는데 각자 공동 호상 동의한다 이 조건과 규정들의 의도는 순전히 군사적 성질에 속하는 것이며 이는 오직 조선에서의 교전 쌍방에만 적용한다

제 1 조
군사 분계선과 비무장 지대

1. 한개의 군사 분계선을 확정하고 쌍방이 이 선으로부터 각기 이 (2) 키로 메터씩 후퇴함으로써 적대 군대간에 한개의 비무장 지대를 설정한다 한개의 비무장 지대를 설정하여 이를 완충 지대로 함으로써 적대 행위의 재발을 초래할 수 있는 사건의 발생을 방지한다

2. 군사 분계선의 위치는 첨부한 지도에 표시한 바와 같다 (첨부한 지도 제1도를 보라)

3. 비무장 지대는 첨부한 지도에 표시한 즉 경계선 및 남 경계선으로써 이를 확정한다 (첨부한 지도 제1도를 보라)

4. 군사 분계선은 하기와 같이 설립한 군사 정전 위원회의 지시에 따라 이를 명백히 표식한다 적대 쌍방 사령관들은 비무장 지대와 각자의 지역간의 경계선에 따라 적당한 표식물을 세운다 군사 정전 위원회는 군사 분계선과 비무장 지대의 각 경계선에 따라 설치한 일체 표식물의 건립을 감독한다

5. 한강 하구의 수역으로서 그 한쪽 강안이 일방의 통제 하에 있고 그 다른 한쪽 강안이 다른 일방의 통제 하에 있는 곳은 쌍방의 민용 선박의 항행에 이를 개방한다 첨부한 지도 (첨부한 지도 제2도를 보라)에서 표시한 부분의 한강 하구의 항행 규칙은 군사 정전 위원회가 이를 규정한다 각방 민용 선박이 항행함에 있어서 자기 측의 군사 통제 하에 있는 육지에 배를 댈 수는 제한받지 않는다

6. 쌍방은 모두 비무장 지대 내에서 또는 비무장 지대로부터 또는 비무장 지대에 향하여 어떠한 적대 행위도 감행하지 못한다

7. 군사 정전 위원회의 특정한 허가없이는 어떠한 군인이나 사민이나

AGREEMENT BETWEEN THE SUPREME COMMANDER OF THE KOREAN PEOPLE'S ARMY AND THE COMMANDER OF THE CHINESE PEOPLE'S VOLUNTEERS, ON THE ONE HAND, AND THE COMMANDER-IN-CHIEF, UNITED NATIONS COMMAND, ON THE OTHER HAND, CONCERNING A MILITARY ARMISTICE IN KOREA

PREAMBLE

The undersigned, the Supreme Commander of the Korean People's Army and the Commander of the Chinese People's Volunteers, on the one hand, and the Commander-in-Chief, United Nations Command, on the other hand, in the interest of stopping the Korean conflict, with its great toll of suffering and bloodshed on both sides, and with the objective of establishing an armistice which will insure a complete cessation of hostilities and of all acts of armed force in Korea until a final peaceful settlement is achieved, do individually, collectively, and mutually agree to accept and to be bound and governed by the conditions and terms of armistice set forth in the following Articles and Paragraphs, which said conditions and terms are intended to be purely military in character and to pertain solely to the belligerents in Korea.

ARTICLE I
MILITARY DEMARCATION LINE AND DEMILITARIZED ZONE

1. A Military Demarcation Line shall be fixed and both sides shall withdraw two (2) kilometers from this line so as to establish a Demilitarized Zone between the opposing forces. A Demilitarized Zone shall be established as a buffer zone to prevent the occurrence of incidents which might lead to a resumption of hostilities.
2. The Military Demarcation Line is located as indicated on the attached map (Map 1).
3. The Demilitarized Zone is defined by a northern and a southern boundary as indicated on the attached map (Map 1).
4. The Military Demarcation Line shall be plainly marked as directed by the Military Armistice Commission hereinafter established. The Commanders of the opposing sides shall have suitable markers erected along the boundary between the Demilitarized Zone and their respective areas. The Military Armistice Commission shall supervise the erection of all markers placed along the Military Demarcation Line and along the boundaries of the Demilitarized Zone.
5. The waters of the Han River Estuary shall be open to civil shipping of both sides wherever one bank is controlled by one side and the other bank is controlled by the other side. The Military Armistice Commission shall prescribe rules for the shipping in that part of the Han River Estuary indicated on the attached map (Map 2). Civil shipping of each side shall have unrestricted access to the land under the military control of that side.

朝鮮人民軍最高司令官及中國人民志願軍司令員一方與聯合國軍總司令另一方
關於朝鮮軍事停戰的協定

序 言

下列簽署人，朝鮮人民軍最高司令官及中國人民志願軍司令員一方，與聯合國軍總司令另一方，為停止造成雙方巨大痛苦與流血的朝鮮衝突，並願在確立最後和平解決以前保證在朝鮮境內敵對行為的停止和一切武裝行動的終止，茲接受下列條款中所載的停戰條件與規定，並擔負受其約束與管制，此等條件與規定純屬軍事性質並僅適用於在朝鮮的交戰雙方。

第一條　軍事分界線與非軍事區

一、確定一軍事分界線，雙方各由此線後退二公里，以便在敵對軍隊之間建立一非軍事區。建立一非軍事區作為緩衝區，以防止可能導致敵對行為再起事件的發生。

二、軍事分界線的位置如附圖所示（見附圖一）。

三、非軍事區以附圖所示的北線與南線確定之（見附圖一）。

四、軍事分界線應接照下述軍事停戰委員會的指示標明白顯。敵對雙方司令官應在非軍事區與其各自地區間的邊沿設立適當標誌。軍事停戰委員會應監督沿軍事分界線與非軍事區兩線設立的總誌物的樹立。

五、漢江江口的水面，其一岸由一方控制而另一岸由另一方控制的，雙方民用船隻均可在其中航行。附圖（見附圖二）所示部分漢江江口的航運規則由軍事停戰委員會規定之。各方民用航運在本方軍事控制下的陸地沿岸靠岸不受限制。

Pyongyang

North Korea

Mapping starts to come together when edited traces of territories come together under an agenda. This is is one of my earliest mapping of the Korean Demilitarized Zone (DMZ) that I made for my research thesis.[1]

Here I start tracing the existing territory to objectively understand the DMZ according to the 1953 Armistice Agreement.

This starts to produce knowledge that become essential ingredients for new imaginations, which start to ask questions such as what is real and what is represented?

매핑은 영토의 편집된 흔적들이 어떤 주제 하에 함께 모일 때 시작한다. 이 매핑은 나의 연구논문에서 가장 초기 매핑 중 하나이다.[1]

여기서 나는 DMZ를 객관적으로 이해하기 위해 1953년 정전협정에 의한 기존 영토와 비무장지대 경계선을 따라 그리기 시작했다.

이 과정은 새로운 상상에 필수 재료가 될 지식을 생산하며, 무엇이 실재하는 현실이고 무엇이 표상된 것인지에 대한 질문으로 시작한다.

Neutral Zone (Han River Estuary)

1.
『Map 001. Line on a Map - The Armistice - The Theoretical Map』in Kim, Dongsei. 2012. 『Border as Urbanism : Redrawing the Demilitarized Zone (DMZ) Between North and South Korea』 (Master's thesis). Harvard University, Graduate School of Design, Cambridge, MA. Page 74.

http://id.lib.harvard.edu/alma/990140527960203941/catalog.

More information at Harvard GSD: https://www.gsd.harvard.edu/project/border-as-urbanism-redrawing-the-demilitarized-zone-dmz-between/

2.
Baudrillard, Jean. 1981/1994. 『Simulacra and Simulation』Ann Arbor: University of Michigan Press.

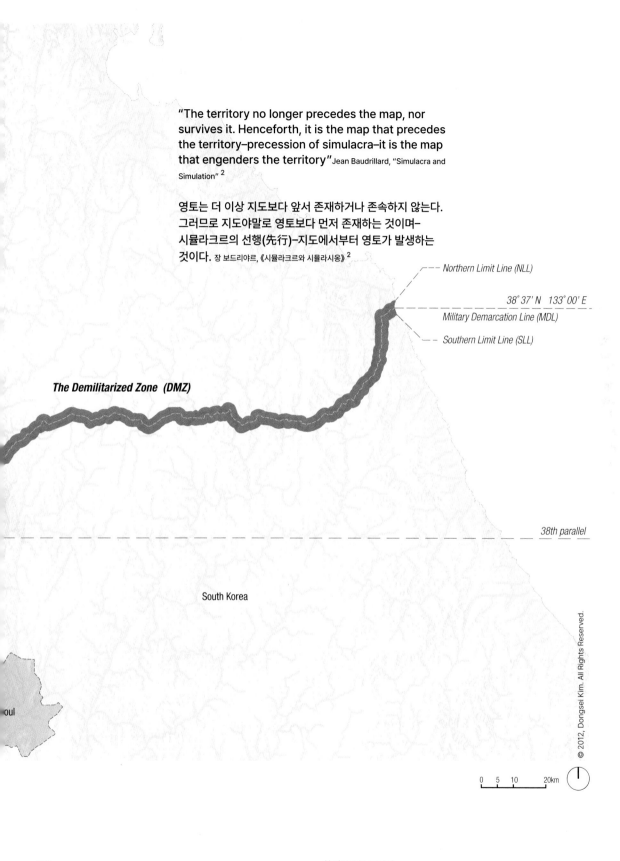

"The territory no longer precedes the map, nor survives it. Henceforth, it is the map that precedes the territory–precession of simulacra–it is the map that engenders the territory" Jean Baudrillard, "Simulacra and Simulation" [2]

영토는 더 이상 지도보다 앞서 존재하거나 존속하지 않는다. 그러므로 지도야말로 영토보다 먼저 존재하는 것이며– 시뮬라크르의 선행(先行)–지도에서부터 영토가 발생하는 것이다. 장 보드리야르, 《시뮬라크르와 시뮬라시옹》 [2]

Northern Limit Line (NLL)

38° 37' N   133° 00' E

Military Demarcation Line (MDL)

Southern Limit Line (SLL)

The Demilitarized Zone (DMZ)

38th parallel

South Korea

oul

0   5   10   20km

화쟁(和諍) 그리기

Deconstructing the DMZ

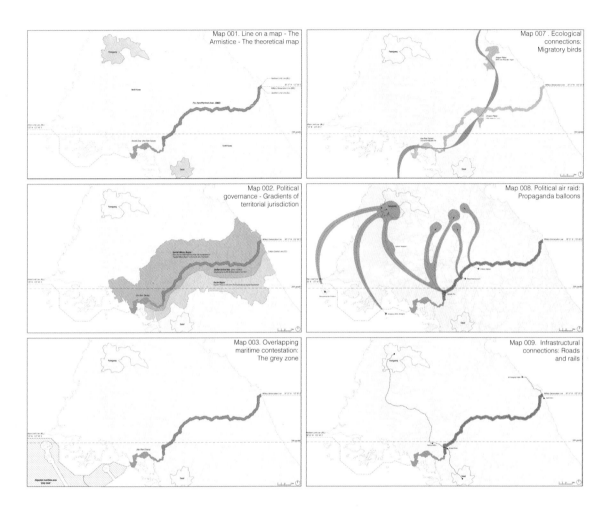

Map 001. Line on a map - The Armistice - The theoretical map

Map 002. Political governance - Gradients of territorial jurisdiction

Map 003. Overlapping maritime contestation: The grey zone

Map 007 . Ecological connections: Migratory birds

Map 008. Political air raid: Propaganda balloons

Map 009 . Infrastructural connections: Roads and rails

The traced DMZ mapping is further deconstructed into layers and visualized to tell new stories. James Corner, in his 『Agency of Mapping』, states:

> the way in which the narrative is assembled, the relating or registering of one thing to another constructs a radically new fiction out of old facts.[2]

기존 지도를 따라 그리는 DMZ 매핑은 새로운 스토리텔링을 위해 여러 층으로 해체되고 시각화된다. 제임스 코너는 《매핑의 힘/역할》에서 다음과 같이 언급한다:

> 어떠한 것을 다른 것들과 연관 짓고 나타내는, 이야기가 접합되는 방식은 기존의 사실을 가지고 근본적이고 새로운 이야기를 만들어낸다.[2]

Drawing Hwa-Chaeng

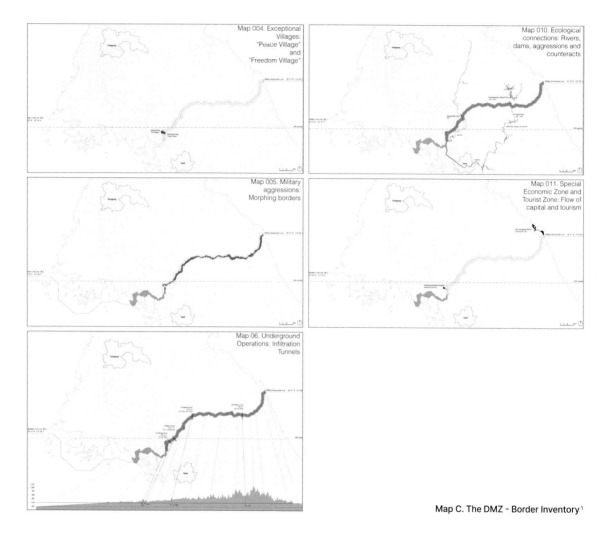

Map C. The DMZ - Border Inventory [1]

1.
Kim, Dongsei. 2012. 『Border as Urbanism : Redrawing the Demilitarized Zone (DMZ) Between North and South Korea』 (Master's thesis). Harvard University, Graduate School of Design, Cambridge, MA. Page 68.

2.
Corner, James. 1999. "The Agency of Mapping: Speculation, Critique and Invention." In 『Mappings』 Edited by Dennis Cosgrove. London: Reaktion Books. Page 239.

Fluctuating Borders Over Time[1]

"Change is the only constant in life"[2]

　　As the saying goes, change is inevitable. The question is who changes what, when, and how. I believe mapping is one unique instrument that allows us to understand how things have changed and how we can imagine their future through a spatio-temporal lens.

　　Diogenes Laërtius further states the following in describing the work of Heraclitus on flux, which talks to dynamics of constant change resulting out of interactions of opposites. "All things come into being by conflict of opposites, and the sum of things (τὰ ὅλα ta hola ("the whole")) flows like a stream."[3]

"인생의 유일한 상수(常數)는 변화다."[2]

　　이 격언이 말하듯 변화란 불가피하다. 문제는 누가 무엇을, 언제, 어떻게 바꾸느냐. 나는 매핑의 특유한 시공간 렌즈를 통해 세상이 어떻게 변해왔는지를 이해하고, 어떻게 미래를 상상할 수 있는지를 이해하게끔 하는 하나의 독특한 도구라고 생각한다.

　　디오게네스 라에르티오스는 헤라클레이토스의 '끊임없는 변화'에 대해 다음과 같이 기술했다. "만물은 상반된 충돌에 의해 생겨나고, 만물의 합은 개울처럼 흐른다."[3]

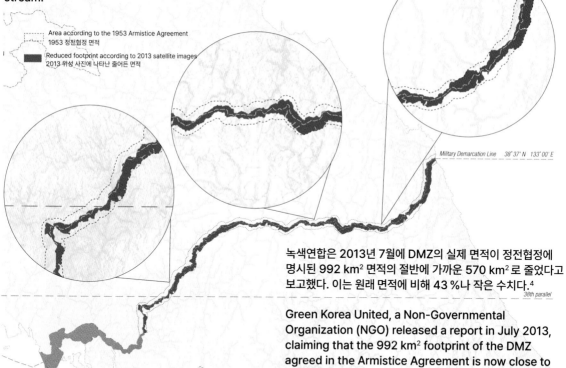

- - - - Area according to the 1953 Armistice Agreement
1953 정전협정 면적

▬ Reduced footprint according to 2013 satellite images
2013 위성 사진에 나타난 줄어든 면적

Military Demarcation Line　38° 37' N　133° 00' E

38th parallel

『Map 005. Military aggressions』[5]

녹색연합은 2013년 7월에 DMZ의 실제 면적이 정전협정에 명시된 992 km² 면적의 절반에 가까운 570 km² 로 줄었다고 보고했다. 이는 원래 면적에 비해 43 %나 작은 수치다.[4]

Green Korea United, a Non-Governmental Organization (NGO) released a report in July 2013, claiming that the 992 km² footprint of the DMZ agreed in the Armistice Agreement is now close to half, standing at 570 km². This is 43% less than the original footprint.[4]

1.
Kim, Dongsei. 2012. 『Border as Urbanism : Redrawing the Demilitarized Zone (DMZ) Between North and South Korea』 (Master's thesis). Harvard University, Graduate School of Design, Cambridge, MA. Page 91.

2.
Heraclitus of Ephesus. Greek philosopher. c. 535 – c. 475 BC.

헤라클레이토스, 고대 그리스의 철학자. c. 535 – c. 475 BC.

3.
Diogenes Laërtius. 『Lives, Teachings, and Sayings of Famous Philosophers』. ix. 8.

디오게네스 라에르티오스.
《유명한 철학자들의 생애와 사상》.

4.
Green Korea. 『2013 DMZ Area Report』 July 23.

녹색연합.
〈2013 년 DMZ 면적 조사보고서〉.

5.
Kim, Dongsei. Ibid., 66.

시간의 흐름에 따라 변하는 경계선[1]

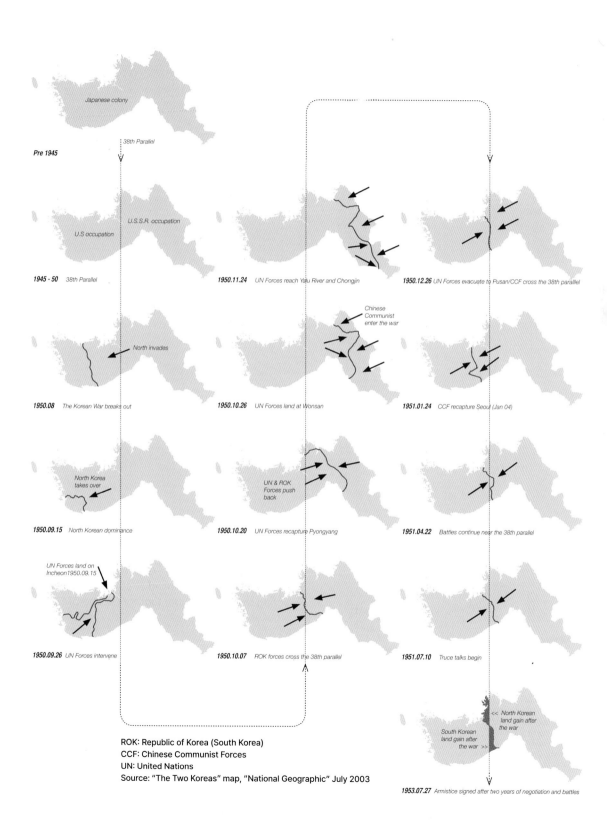

Japanese colony

38th Parallel

Pre 1945

1945 - 50   *38th Parallel*

U.S.S.R. occupation

U.S occupation

1950.08   *The Korean War breaks out*

North invades

1950.09.15   *North Korean dominance*

North Korea takes over

1950.09.26   *UN Forces intervene*

UN Forces land on Incheon1950.09.15

1950.11.24   *UN Forces reach Yalu River and Chongjin*

1950.10.26   *UN Forces land at Wonsan*

Chinese Communist enter the war

1950.10.20   *UN Forces recapture Pyongyang*

UN & ROK Forces push back

1950.10.07   *ROK forces cross the 38th parallel*

1950.12.26   *UN Forces evacuate to Pusan/CCF cross the 38th paralllel*

1951.01.24   *CCF recapture Seoul (Jan 04)*

1951.04.22   *Battles continue near the 38th parallel*

1951.07.10   *Truce talks begin*

<< North Korean land gain after the war

South Korean land gain after the war >>

1953.07.27   *Armistice signed after two years of negotiation and battles*

ROK: Republic of Korea (South Korea)
CCF: Chinese Communist Forces
UN: United Nations
Source: "The Two Koreas" map, "National Geographic" July 2003

The Demilitarized Zone: Redrawing the 151 mile Border between North and South Korea

Four ways of seeing the DMZ [1]

HISTORY OF THE DMZ

Korean War 1950.06.25   1953.07.27   2012   1896

Detector Trends
NUMBER OF CUMULATIVE
NORTH KOREAN DEFECTORS
IN SOUTH KOREA

19,964
17,986
15,059
12,250
9,706
7,698
6,305
4,411
3,130
1,991

Clandestine Routes -
only about 30% make it to
their final destination
3,000 mile (4,000km) clandestine journey

Harbin, Heilongjiang
Jilin, Jilin
Beijing
Shenyang, Liaoning
Hanoi, Vietnam
Vientiane, Laos
Yangon, Burma
Bangkok, Thailand
Phnom Penh, Cambodia
Ho Chi Minh, Vietnam

DMZ IN GLOBAL FLUX

Within the global context the meaning and role of the DMZ becomes more obvious. North Korea is one of only five communist states, this means it is a communist-capitalist borderline, dubbed the "bamboo curtain." In regards to its economic standing and welfare, it is a global south and north borderline. Geopolitically, the Korean peninsula has been the frontiers for expanding the Mongols, China, Japan, Russia and U.S. The DMZ is more than a border between North and South Korea. It represents tensions and contrasts in ideologies and politics.

The heavily fortified 151-mile DMZ gives rise to the 3,000 miles clandestine journey, escaping the North Korea. Two-six months to several years journey has been taken up by almost 25,000 North Koreans. They travel through China, and many other South East Asian countries eventually defecting to South

Korea. Some make it to the U.S. and other Western countries. This one prime example of how these border conditions externalize the effects in unexpected processes. Many do not make it to the South and are captured and sent back to political concentration camps in North Korea, or become long-term illegal overstayers in China, often abused. Understanding this dynamic forces and nature of the DMZ enables us to construct alternative perspectives that spark forward moving dialogues.

NUMBER OF NORTH KOREAN DEFECTORS PER YEAR

2,927
2,809
2,544
2,013
1,894
1,383
1,281
1,139
583
312
148
71
56
41
633   641   693   734   790   677   948   1,096   1,408

1.
Kim, Dongsei; 2012. 『Border as Urbanism : Redrawing the Demilitarized Zone (DMZ) Between North and South Korea』 (Master's thesis). Harvard University, Graduate School of Design, Cambridge, MA. Page 58-61.

Barriers / 장애물

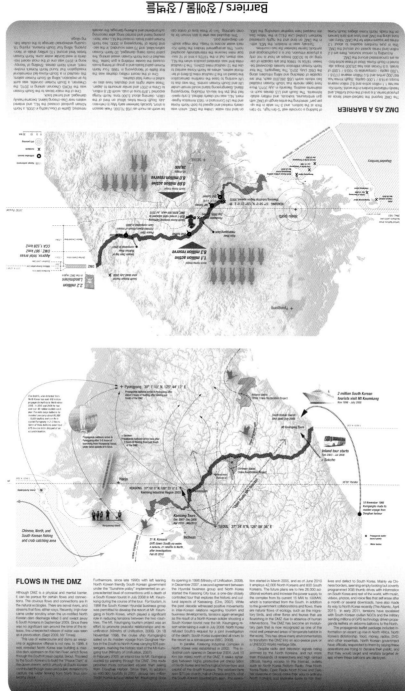

Flows / 이동과 흐름들

DMZ를 바라보는 네 가지 관점 [1]

FLOWS IN THE DMZ

A Construct The Koreas (Never) Made Together: Deconstructing the DMZ For The Imaginary — A

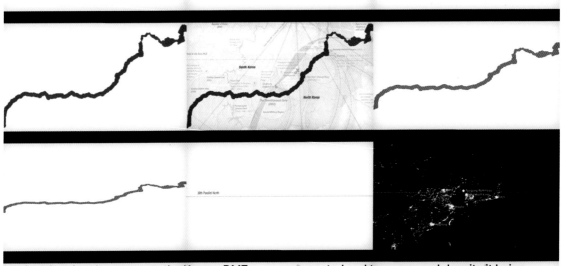

This animation deconstructs the Korean DMZ through five lenses. The first lens examines the DMZ through history and illustrates how the DMZ fluctuates over time. The second lens demonstrates how the DMZ functions as a solid barrier that reinforces divided Korea. The third lens reveals how the DMZ is connected and transgressed despite it being an impenetrable barrier. The fourth lens zooms out its point of view out to Northeast Asia to trace North Koreans who partake in the 5,000-km clandestine escape route. The last lens elucidates how the two Koreas are starting to deconstruct the Cold War border.[1]

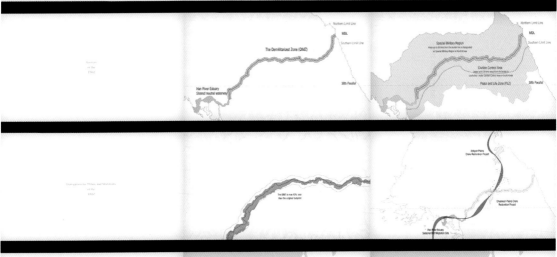

1.
This text description is from the 2019 iteration. The original research animation 『A Construct The Koreas (Never) Made Together Deconstructing the DMZ For The Imaginary』 assisted by Namju Lee and Eleni Gianpapa was exhibited in the Golden Lion award-winning 『Crow's Eye View: The Korean Peninsula』 exhibition curated by Minsuk Cho, Hyungmin Pai, and Changmo Ahn with deputy Curator Jihoi Lee at the 14th International Architecture Exhibition in 2014.

This animation was revised and invited to the 『DMZ』 exhibition curated by Sunjung Kim, Haeju Kim, SooJin Lee, Miyeon Jun, Kyungjin Zoh, Heehyun Cho, and Keum Hyun Han at Culture Station Seoul 284 in 2019.

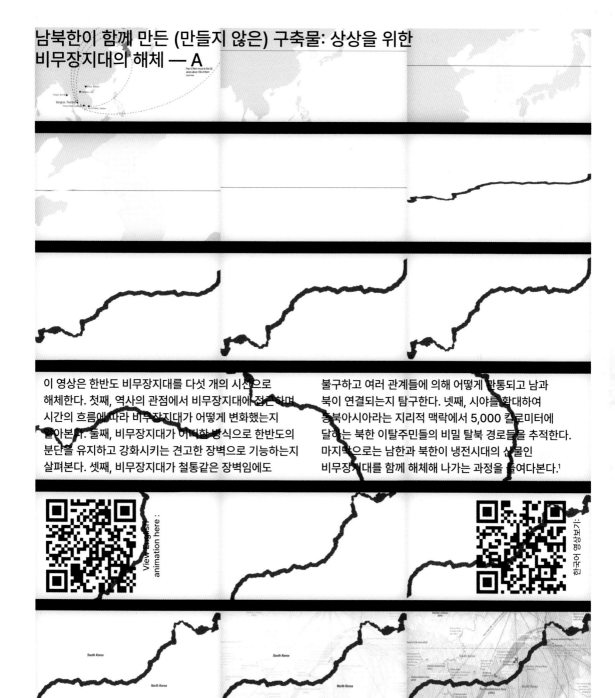

이 영상은 한반도 비무장지대를 다섯 개의 시선으로 해체한다. 첫째, 역사의 관점에서 비무장지대에 접근하며 시간의 흐름에따라 비무장지대가 어떻게 변화했는지 알아본다. 둘째, 비무장지대가 어떠한 방식으로 한반도의 분단을 유지하고 강화시키는 견고한 장벽으로 기능하는지 살펴본다. 셋째, 비무장지대가 철통같은 장벽임에도 불구하고 여러 관계들에 의해 어떻게 관통되고 남과 북이 연결되는지 탐구한다. 넷째, 시야를 확대하여 동북아시아라는 지리적 맥락에서 5,000 킬로미터에 달하는 북한 이탈주민들의 비밀 탈북 경로들을 추적한다. 마지막으로는 남한과 북한이 냉전시대의 산물인 비무장지대를 함께 해체해 나가는 과정을 들여다본다.[1]

View English animation here :

국문 영상 보기 :

The Demilitarized Zone Timeline in Longue Durée

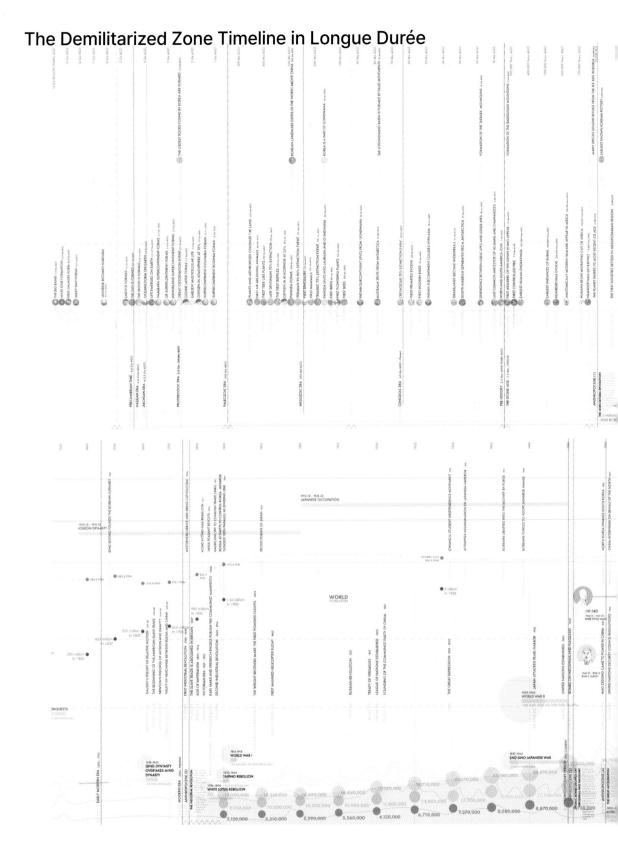

장기 지속의 비무장지대 연대기 (年代記)

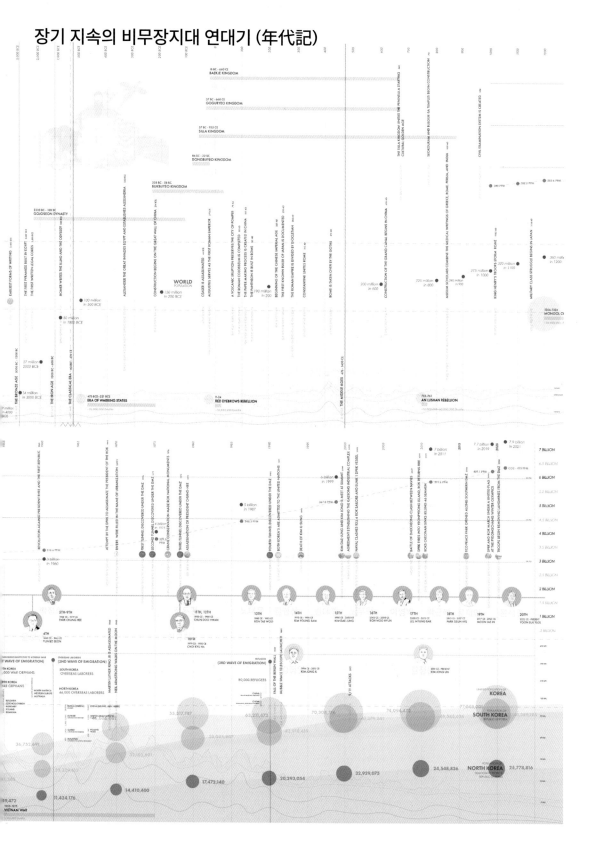

How large is the DMZ? What if the DMZ was a...

Seoul
605.3 km² / 233.7 mi²
9.8 M (2017)
16,152 inhabitants/km²
41,833 inhabitants/mi²

Berlin
891.7 km² / 344.3 mi²
3.6 M inhabitants (2020)
4,087 inhabitants/km²
10,586 inhabitants/mi²

Pyongyang
2,000 km² / 772.2 mi²
2.9 M inhabitants (2016)
1,450 inhabitants/km²
3,756 inhabitants/mi²

Han River Estuary

Han River Estuary

Time taken to travel along the 240 km (150 mi) DMZ.

Walking (4.8 km/h | 3 mi/h) — 50 hours

Biking (20 km/h | 12 mi/h) — 12.5 hours

The Demilitarized Zone (DMZ)

992 km² 383 mi²
193 inhabitants (2018)
0.195 inhabitants/km² | 0.5 inhabitants/mi²

DMZ is an approximately 250 km (148 miles) long & 4 km (2.5 miles) wide
military–infrastructural landscape
The agreed area in the 1953 Armistice Agreement is approximately
992 km² (245,129 acres)

The DMZ's footprint in reality

According to Green Korea's report (2018)
the DMZ's footprint is close to 570 km² | 220 mi²
(57% of original footprint) due to military agressions on the ground

The DMZ's area is equivalent to...
1.5 x of **Seoul**, **1/2** of **Pyongyang**
& **291 Central Parks** (843 acres)

Singapore

728.6 km² / 281.3 mi²
5.7 M inhabitants (2020)
7,804 inhabitants/km²
20,213 inhabitants/mi²

New York City

1,223.6 km² / 302.6 mi²
8.8 M inhabitants (2020)
6,880 inhabitants/km²
27,822 inhabitants/mi²

Driving — 2.5 hours (100 km/h | 60 mi/h)

Flying — 20 minutes (800 km/h | 500 mi/h)

0   5   10   20km   12.5 mi

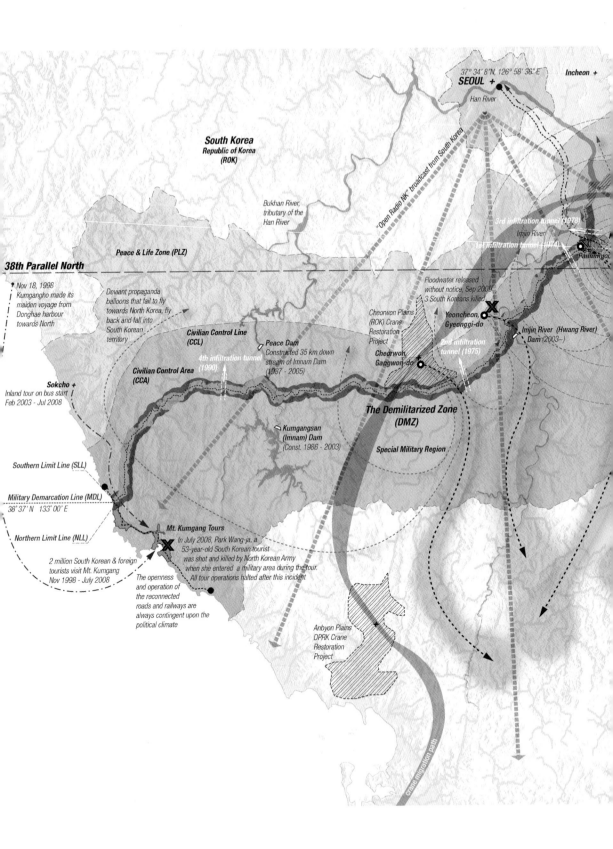

37° 34' 8"N, 126° 58' 36" E
SEOUL +   Incheon +
Han River

South Korea
Republic of Korea
(ROK)

Bukhan River,
tributary of the
Han River

"Open Radio NK" broadcast from South Korea

3rd Infiltration tunnel (1978)

Imjin River

1st Infiltration tunnel (1974)

Panmunjeom

Peace & Life Zone (PLZ)

– – – **38th Parallel North** – – – – – – – – – – – – – – – – – – –

Nov 18, 1998
Kumgangho made its
maiden voyage from
Donghae harbour
towards North

Deviant propaganda
balloons that fail to fly
towards North Korea, fly
back and fall into
South Korean
territory

Floodwater released
without notice, Sep 2009.
3 South Koreans killed

Cheorwon Plains
(ROK) Crane
Restoration
Project

**Yeoncheon,
Gyeonggi-do**

Imjin River (Hwang River)
Dam (2003~)

**Civilian Control Line
(CCL)**

4th infiltration tunnel
(1990)

Peace Dam
Constructed 35 km down
stream of Imnam Dam
(1987 - 2005)

**Cheorwon,
Gangwon-do**

2nd infiltration
tunnel (1975)

**Civilian Control Area
(CCA)**

Sokcho +
Inland tour on bus start
Feb 2003 - Jul 2008

Kumgangsan
(Imnam) Dam
(Const. 1986 - 2003)

**The Demilitarized Zone
(DMZ)**

Special Military Region

Southern Limit Line (SLL)

Military Demarcation Line (MDL)
38° 37' N 133° 00' E

Northern Limit Line (NLL)

Mt. Kumgang Tours
In July 2008, Park Wang-ja, a
53-year-old South Korean tourist
was shot and killed by North Korean Army
when she entered a military area during the tour.
All tour operations halted after this incident

2 million South Korean & foreign
tourists visit Mt. Kumgang
Nov 1998 - July 2008

The openness
and operation of
the reconnected
roads and railways are
always contingent upon the
political climate

Anbyon Plains
DPRK Crane
Restoration
Project

crane migration path

Drawing Hwa-Chaeng

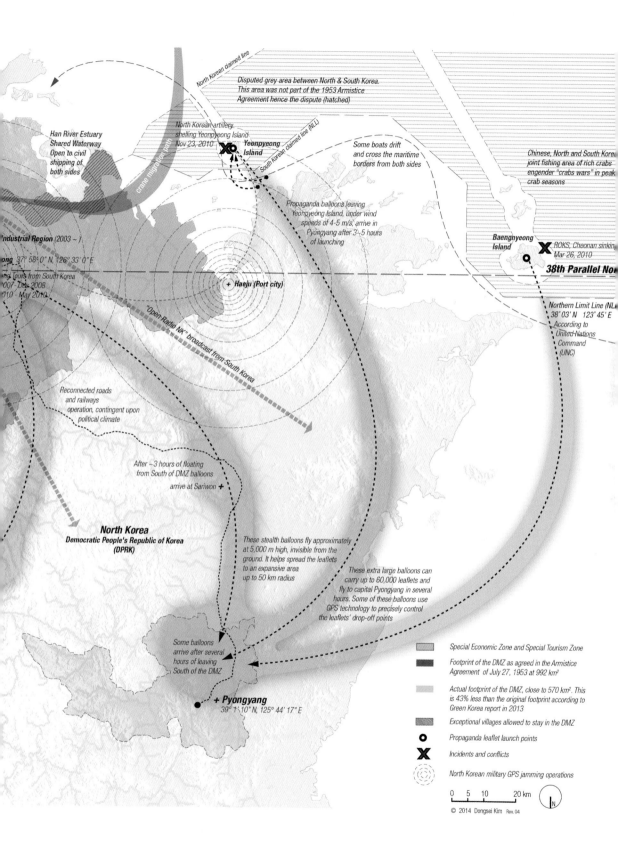

Han River Estuary
Shared Waterway
Open to civil
shipping of
both sides

North Korean claimed line

Disputed grey area between North & South Korea.
This area was not part of the 1953 Armistice
Agreement hence the dispute (hatched)

North Korean artillery
shelling Yeonpyeong Island
Nov 23, 2010

Yeonpyeong
Island

South Korean claimed line (NLL)

Some boats drift
and cross the maritime
borders from both sides

Chinese, North and South Korea
joint fishing area of rich crabs
engender "crabs wars" in peak
crab seasons

Industrial Region (2003 ~)

ong 37° 58' 0" N, 126° 33' 0" E

ng Tours from South Korea
007 - Dec 2008
010 - May 2010)

Propaganda balloons leaving
Yeonpyeong Island, under wind
speeds of 4-5 m/s, arrive in
Pyöngyang after 3~5 hours
of launching

Baengnyeong
Island

ROKS, Cheonan sinking
Mar 26, 2010

38th Parallel Nor

+ Haeju (Port city)

"Open Radio NK" broadcast from South Korea

Northern Limit Line (NL
38° 03' N 123° 45' E
According to
United Nations
Command
(UNC)

Reconnected roads
and railways
operation, contingent upon
political climate

After ~3 hours of floating
from South of DMZ balloons
arrive at Sariwon +

North Korea
Democratic People's Republic of Korea
(DPRK)

These stealth balloons fly approximately
at 5,000 m high, invisible from the
ground. It helps spread the leaflets
to an expansive area
up to 50 km radius

These extra large balloons can
carry up to 60,000 leaflets and
fly to capital Pyongyang in several
hours. Some of these balloons use
GPS technology to precisely control
the leaflets' drop-off points

Some balloons
arrive after several
hours of leaving
South of the DMZ

+ Pyongyang
39° 1' 10" N, 125° 44' 17" E

Special Economic Zone and Special Tourism Zone

Footprint of the DMZ as agreed in the Armistice
Agreement of July 27, 1953 at 992 km²

Actual footprint of the DMZ, close to 570 km². This
is 43% less than the original footprint according to
Green Korea report in 2013

Exceptional villages allowed to stay in the DMZ

Propaganda leaflet launch points

Incidents and conflicts

North Korean military GPS jamming operations

0   5   10   20 km

N

© 2014 Dongsei Kim Rev. 04

crane migration path

A Construct The Koreas (Never) Made Together: Deconstructing the DMZ For The Imaginary[1] — B

Imagining the Impossible: Projecting the DMZ's Future(s) [2]

1. _What if the DMZ_ was an **Energy Farm?** Flows of solar, hydro, wind power and their potentials.
2. _What if the DMZ_ was an **Ecological field?** Flows of migratory birds, animals, disease etc.
3. _What if the DMZ_ was a **Special Economic Zone?** Flows of capital, people and money.
4. _What if the DMZ_ was a **Transportation Hub?** Flows of people associated with transportation.
5. _What if the DMZ_ was a **Special Tourism Zone?** Flows of people, meeting of separated families etc.
6. _What if the DMZ_ was a **Military Base for the unified Korea?** Flows of military industrial complex.
7. _What if the DMZ_ was a **Food producing agricultural fields?**
8. _What if the DMZ_ was a **High-tech hub?**
9. _What if the DMZ_ was a **UNESCO heritage Site? UN Asia Office?**

What else?

1.
『A Constrcut the Koreas (Never) Made Together: Deconstucting the DMZ for the Imaginary』 2014, (Video, 08:24) was exhibited at the Golden Lion Award Winning 『Crow's Eye View: The Korean Peninsula』, curated by Minsuk Cho, Hyungmin Pai, & Changmo Ahn at the 14th International Architecture Exhibition in Venice, Italy directed by Rem Koolhaas.

More detail can be found at: Kim, Dongsei. 2014. 『A Construct the Koreas (Never) Made Together: Deconstructing the DMZ for the Imaginary.』 In 『Crow's Eye View: The Korean Peninsula 』 edited by Hyungmin Pai and Minsuk Cho, 192-194. Seoul: Archilife. (ISBN 978-89-964508-6-3 93610)

2.
Excerpt from 『What If The DMZ Became a...? Imagining the Impossible』, Master of Landscape Architecture (MLA) Upper Pool: Design Research Studio brief at RMIT University, 2015 instructed by author.

3.
Paik, Nak-Chung. 『Forward』 to the Korean-Language Edition 『The Division System in Crisis: Essays on Contemporary Korea』 (Berkeley: University of California Press, 2011), xiii-xiv.

남북한이 함께 만든 (만들지 않은) 구축물: 상상을 위한 비무장지대의 해체[1] — B

This mapping project is inspired by Uruguayan artist Joaquín Torres García who declared "Our North is the South".

His 『América Invertida』 (1943) depicts South America with the South on top instead of the conventional North on top.

『América Invertida』 critiques European colonization of the Americas and 『A Construct the Koreas (Never) Made Together: Deconstructing the DMZ for the Imaginary』[1] comments on the imperial powers at play in the Korean Peninsula.

이 매핑 프로젝트는 우루과이의 예술가 호아킨 토레스 가르시아가 "우리의 북쪽은 남쪽이다."라고 선언한 것에서 영감을 얻어 시작되었다.

그의 "도치된 남미 지도"(1943)는 북쪽을 위에 두는 전통적인 지도에서와 달리 남쪽이 위로 향하는 남미대륙을 묘사하고 있다.

"도치된 남미 지도"는 유럽의 아메리카 식민지화를 비판하고, "남북한이 함께 만든 (만들지 않은) 구축물: 상상을 위한 비무장지대의 해체"[1]는 한반도에서 벌어지고 있는 제국주의 세력에 대해 논평한다.

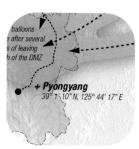

… in discussing the division system (division of the Korean peninsula) is to show that we must free ourselves from the obsession for finding "*the* correct answer." Such obsession certainly is not confined to the issue of the division system, but I believe that the crucial part of the project for overcoming the division system consists in willingly undertaking efforts for self-exploration and self-renewal, based upon a keen recognition that the very consciousness of those who believe they have the correct answers for overcoming the division is seriously distorted by that system.[3]

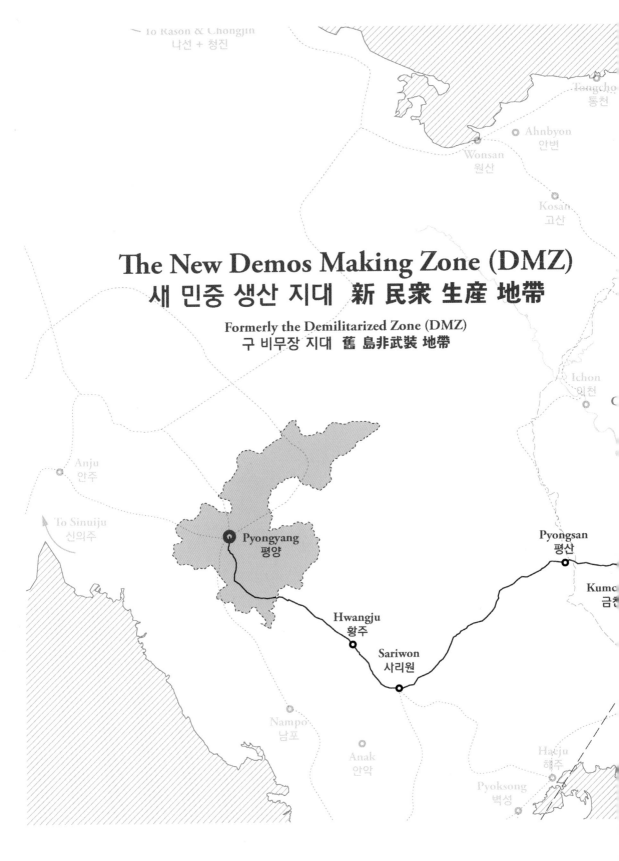

The New Demos Making Zone (DMZ)
새 민중 생산 지대 新 民衆 生産 地帶

Formerly the Demilitarized Zone (DMZ)
구 비무장 지대 舊 島非武裝 地帶

To Kason & Chongjin
나선 + 청진

Tongcho
통천

Ahnbyon
안변

Wonsan
원산

Kosan
고산

Ichon
이천

Anju
안주

To Sinuiju
신의주

Pyongyang
평양

Pyongsan
평산

Kumc
금천

Hwangju
황주

Sariwon
사리원

Nampo
남포

Anak
안악

Haeju
해주

Pyoksong
벽성

Drawing Hwa-Chaeng

Mount Kumgang
금강산
+ 1,638 m (5,374 ft)

Kosung
고성

Sokcho
속초

Yangyang
양양

Gangneung
강릉

Dong
동해

Kumgang
금강

Mount Seorak
설악산
+ 1,708 m (5,604 ft)

Mount Odae
오대산
+ 1,563 m (5,128 ft)

Jeongse
정선

Changdo
창도

Inje
인제

Pyeongchang
평창

Yanggu
양구

Pyonggang
평강

Hwacheon
화천

Chuncheon
춘천

Hongcheon
홍천

Hoengseong
횡성

Cheorwon
철원

Wonju
원주

won
원

Yeoncheon
연천

Pochun
포천

Yangpyeong
양평

To Daegu & Busan
대구 + 부산

Namynagju
남양주

Ujieongbu
의정부

Paju
파주

Goyang
고양

Seoul
서울

Seongnam
성남

To Sejong + Daeje
세종 + 대전

Kaesong
개성

Suwon
수원

Gimpo
김포

Ansan
안산

Incheon
인천

Ganghwa
강화

To Gwang
광주

Yonan
연안

38th pa

0 5 10   20   40   60   80   100 km

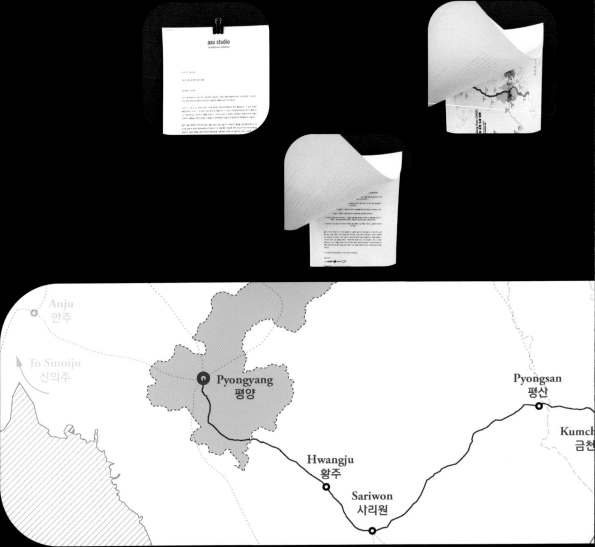

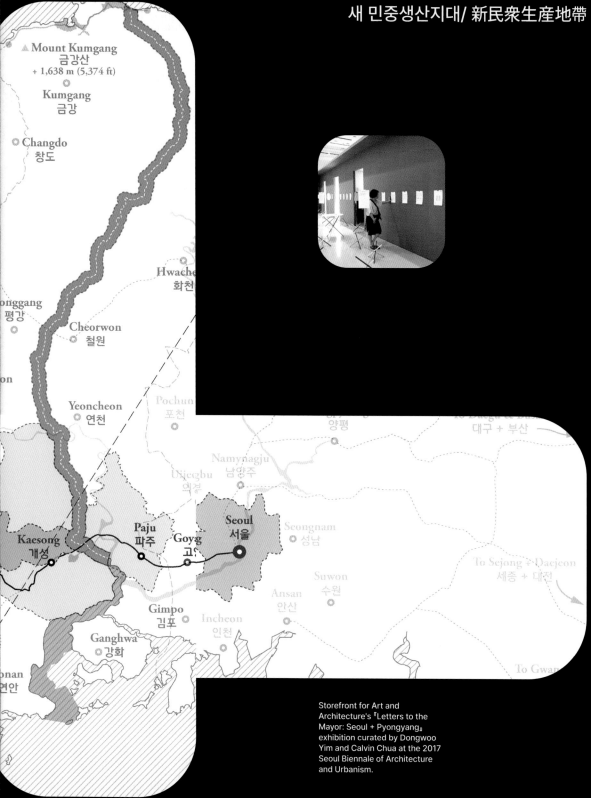

Storefront for Art and
Architecture's 『Letters to the
Mayor: Seoul + Pyongyang』
exhibition curated by Dongwoo
Yim and Calvin Chua at the 2017
Seoul Biennale of Architecture
and Urbanism.

axu studio
architecture x urbanism
e: info@axustudio.com w: axustudio.com

November 30, 2019

RE: The New DMZ: A Proposition

Dear Mayor of Pyongyang—Seoul,

Congratulations on being elected to the first Mayor of Pyongyang—Seoul! It is certainly an exciting time for Pyongyang and Seoul. In fact, it is a time of monumental transition for the entire Korean Peninsula and Northeast Asia.

On November 9, 2019, the gates of the Demilitarized Zone (DMZ) between North and South Korea opened. It was the same day when the Germans were celebrating the 30th anniversary of the fall of the Berlin Wall. Nobody anticipated the gates of the DMZ to open so suddenly. However, many anticipated this unprecedented move to be inevitable considering the new geopolitical conditions of Northeast Asia that emerged in early 2018.

While there are many important things to be done for Pyongyang and Seoul itself, I believe there are much more important matters to consider when we put both cities into the larger context of the early stages of the Korean unification process. One recommendation I have for you as the first Mayor of Pyongyang—Seoul is to work in close collaboration with the Korean Government to consider the DMZ as an integral part of the Pyongyang—Seoul megaregion. This transitionary period we have is a rare opportunity we should seize. I want to reemphasize that the DMZ should be an integral part of any discussion when Pyongyang and Seoul are discussed as a pair.

First, I suggest naming this region the New Demos Making Zone (DMZ). A place where its ordinary citizens (demos) are given priority over capital. Please see the attached map. What exactly happens in the DMZ, and what kind of relationship it has to Pyongyang and Seoul should be first put forward to the public.

On that note, I would like to share some of my thoughts on the DMZ and its region based on my ongoing research. Below is a revised "non-manifesto for the DMZ," I wrote in 2014. Please have a look and use it as a reference for my recommendations. I hope this can become a basis for developing a holistic agenda for the New DMZ, Pyongyang and Seoul.

< A non-manifesto for the DMZ >, 2014*

1. The South Korean President Park wants a Peace Park in the DMZ. *It should be more than a mere Peace Park.*

2. The DMZ should be first *deconstructed and deeply understood,* not prematurely "designed."

3. The DMZ should be about *"to design the conditions"* rather than *"to condition the design"* (Borrowing from Bernard Tschumi's "Architecture and Disjuncture," 6).

4. The DMZ should learn from Marcel Duchamp's "Fountain-Urinal," from the spirit of objet trouvé.

5. No single individual or single organization should dictate what the DMZ should be; it should be a *conduit for collective imaginations.*

6. The DMZ should be *productive.* It should *produce food, energy, waste, economy, culture, value, vision, and more.*

7. The DMZ should be *"more and more, more is more"* (Borrowing from Rem Koolhaas).

8. The DMZ should *question hegemony: power, control, and greed.*

9. The "DMZ MUST BECOME A TIGER FARM. 1. TO ATTRACT JAPANESE TOURISTS. 2. TO KEEP ECOLOGY HEAVEN 3. TO EAT UP INVADORS. [sic]" (Borrowing from Nam June Paik, Project DMZ, 1998).

10. What is the most important thing in the DMZ? *It is the people, it is the people, it is the people* (Borrowing from a New Zealand Maori proverb).

Of course, these short statements are just a starting point. Nonetheless, I believe they embody important principles of a good city and a region, mainly of a city that prioritizes its citizens, the collective, and the public over capital. I agree, it is a sure simple statement to make, but an immensely difficult task to execute. Because it is such a difficult task, it is important that we come together and proactively discuss these future scenarios through various open platforms. I strongly believe architects have a great role in envisioning a better future for this new megapolis. I hope my view on the New DMZ will help you to lead both Pyongyang and Seoul in conjunction with the New DMZ to a better future.

Congratulations again, and I look forward to meeting you soon.

Yours sincerely,

Dongsei Kim ANZIA, RA, MDesS(Dist), MSAUD, B.Arch(Hons)
Founder, **axu studio**
dongsei@axustudio.com

* Edited excerpt from: Kim, Dongsei. 2014. "A Construct the Koreas (never) made together: Deconstructing the DMZ for the Imaginary" In *North Korea Atlas*, edited by Dongwoo Yim and Rafael Luna, p566-571. Seoul: Damdi.

2019 년 11 월 30 일

새로운 DMZ 에 대한 하나의 제안

서울-평양 시장님께,

우선 서울-평양의 첫 시장이 되신 것을 축하 드립니다! 지금은 서울과 평양에 있어서 가장 중요한 시기입니다. 사실 전(全) 한반도와 동북아시아에 있어 기념비적인 변화의 순간이기도 합니다.

2019 년 11 월 9 일, 북한과 남한 사이에 위치한 비무장지대(DMZ)의 문이 열렸습니다. 이 날은 독일의 베를린장벽이 무너진 지 30 주년이 되던 날이기도 했습니다. 그 누구도 비무장지대(DMZ)의 문이 그렇게 한 순간 열리리라고는 생각하지 못했을 것입니다. 하지만 2018 년 초부터 감지되었던 동북아시아의 새로운 지정학적 상황들을 고려한다면 많은 사람들은 이 전대미문의 사건을 이미 필연적으로 예견했을지도 모릅니다.

물론 서울과 평양에서 해야 할 중요한 일들이 많이 있을 것입니다. 하지만 막 통일을 이룬 한반도에서 이 두 도시들 앞에 더 중요한 일에 놓여있다고 믿습니다. 첫 서울-평양 시장님께 제가 드리고자 하는 하나의 제안은 정부와의 긴밀한 협력을 통해 비무장지대(DMZ)를 서울-평양 거대도시의 필수적인 공간이 되도록 하자는 것입니다. 이 과도기적 시기는 반드시 붙잡아야 할 흔치 않은 기회가 될 것입니다. 서울과 평양을 하나로 묶어 논의할 때 DMZ 역시 이에 중요한 부분으로 함께 논의되어야 한다는 사실을 다시 한번 강조하고 싶습니다.

우선 저는 이 공간을 "새 민중 생산 지대/新 民衆 生産 地帶 (New Demos Making Zone: New DMZ)"라고 명명할 것을 제안합니다. 사람과 공동체가 자본보다 우선시 되는 그런 곳을 말하는 것입니다. 이 공간에 대해서는 첨부된 지도를 참고해주십시요. DMZ 에서 무슨 일이 일어나고 있으며, 서울, 평양과 어떤 연관을 이어갈지 이러한 사안들은 대중에게 먼저 제안하고 알려야 할 것입니다.

이와 관련하여, 제가 현재 진행하고 있는 연구를 바탕으로 DMZ 와 그 주변 지역에 대한 저희 견해를 나누고자 합니다. 아래에 있는 글은 제가 2014 년도에 작성한 「DMZ 를 위한 비(非)선언문」의 수정본 입니다. 한 번 살펴보시고 저의 건의사항에 대한 참고자료로 사용해주시기 바랍니다. 이 자료가 새로운 DMZ, 서울 그리고 평양에 대한 전체적인 계획을 수립하는 데에 기초가 될 수 있기를 바랍니다.

「DMZ를 위한 비(非)선언문」, 2014*

1. 대한민국의 박근혜 대통령(당시 대통령)은 DMZ 내 평화공원을 추진하기를 바라지만 그곳은 단순한 평화공원 그 이상이 되어야 한다.

2. DMZ는 급조해서 "계획" 되어서는 안되며 심도 있는 해체와 이해를 필요로 한다.

3. DMZ는 "디자인의 조건을 결정"하는 것이 아닌, "상황과 조건을 디자인"하는 것에 초점을 맞추어야 한다.
(베르나르 츄미, 「건축과 해체」, 6 페이지 인용)

4. DMZ는 마르셀 뒤샹의 작품 <샘>, 즉 오브제 트루베(objet trouvé)의 정신을 배워야 한다.

5. DMZ가 무엇이 되어야 하는지에 대한 논의는 어느 한 개인이나 하나의 기관에 의해 좌우되어서는 안 된다.
이 공간은 공동체의 상상력이 발현되는 곳이어야 한다.

6. DMZ는 생산적이어야 한다. 이 공간은 식량, 에너지, 쓰레기, 경제, 문화, 가치, 비전 등을 생산해낼 수 있어야 한다.

7. DMZ는 "더 그리고 더, 많음이 그 이상이다 (다다익선, 多多益善)"를 지향하여야 한다 (렘 쿨하스 인용).

8. DMZ는 헤게모니, 권력, 통제 그리고 탐욕에 대한 문제의식을 지녀야 한다.

9. DMZ는 호랑이 농장이 되어야 한다. 1. 일본인 관광객들을 끌어들이기 위해서 2. 생태천국을 유지하기 위해서 3. 침략자들을 잡아먹기 위해서. (백남준의 <프로젝트 DMZ> (1998 년) 인용)

10. DMZ에서 가장 소중한 것이 무엇인가? 첫째도 사람, 둘째도 사람, 셋째도 사람이다. (뉴질랜드 마오리족 격언 인용)

물론 이 간단한 제안들은 그저 시작에 불과합니다. 그럼에도 불구하고 이것이 좋은 도시, 지방, 특히 그곳에 살게 되는 시민들, 공동체, 그리고 공공(公共)을 우선시하는 도시를 구축하기 위해 반드시 인지하고 수용해야 하는 원칙들이라고 믿습니다. 이것은 말보다는 실천하기에 대단히 어려운 과제들이라는 사실에 동의합니다. 그러기에 다양한 오픈 플랫폼을 통해 이 미래를 함께 협의해 나가는 것이 중요합니다. 저는 이 새로운 거대도시의 더 나은 미래를 그려내는 데에 건축가들의 역할이 중요하다고 믿습니다. 새 DMZ에 대한 저의 견해가 새로운 DMZ와 함께 서울과 평양 모두를 더 나은 미래로 이끌어가고자 하는 시장님께 도움이 되기를 바랍니다.

다시 한번 축하의 말씀을 전합니다. 그리고 곧 뵐 수 있길 빕니다.

김동세 드림

Dongsei Kim ANZIA, RA, MDesS(Dist), MSAUD, B.Arch(Hons)
Founder, **axu studio**
dongsei@axustudio.com

*수정 발췌: 김동세, 「남북한이 함께 만든(만들지 않은) 구축물: 상상을 위한 비무장지대의 해체」, 「북한 도시 읽기」, 임동우, 라파엘 루나 엮음. 서울: 담디, 2014.
566-571. <한글 번역: 최이수>

Seeing is Believing (Way of Seeing & Scale)

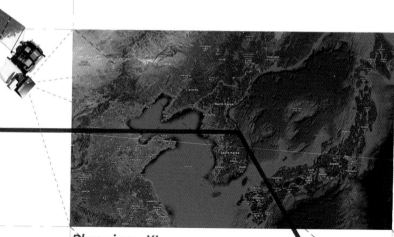

Plan view - XL

Oblique view - L / M

"Seeing is believing, thus understanding." This drawing illustrates how the Korean Demilitarized Zone (DMZ) is understood through three different points of view and scales.

The first representation of the DMZ is constructed through satellite imaging technology. Small-scale plan views of the DMZ are produced from satellites such as the NASA/USGS Landsat 8 that hover 705 km (438 miles) above the earth's surface.

The second oblique view of the DMZ operates at a medium scale, a view afforded from a hilltop or a flying drone (120 m/400 ft).

Finally, the on-the-ground perspective image engages personal experiences at an intimate scale. The author took this photo during one of the field trips to the DMZ in 2011.

These three images at varying scales represent different parts of the DMZ. Generated through a set of matching technologies from a range of distances from the DMZ, they start to produce multiple readings of the DMZ.

It further points to the fact that multiple views can produce multiple meanings and stories of an identical object or phenomenon.

Timeline   << Long-term   << Mid-term >>

보이는 것을 믿다(보는 방식과 스케일)

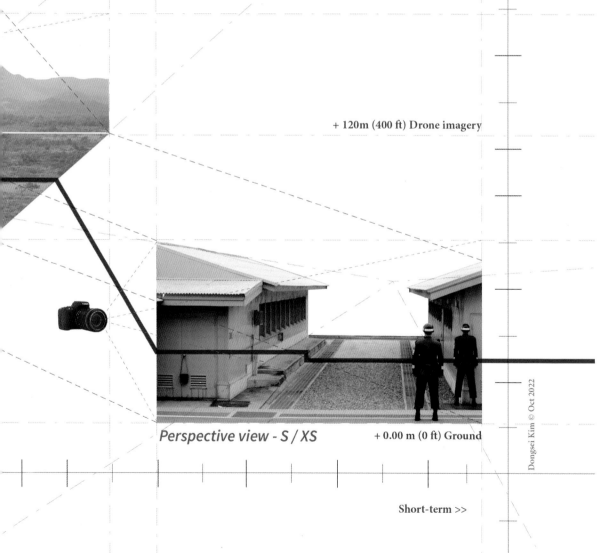

Elevation/ Scale

+ 705 km (438 mi) NASA/USGS Landsat 8 Satellite imagery (2013 -)

"보는 것은 믿는 것이고, 따라서 이해하는 것이다." 이 드로잉은 세 가지 다른 관점과 척도를 통해 비무장지대 (DMZ)가 어떻게 이해되는지를 보여준다.

첫 번째 이미지는 위성 영상 기술을 통해 구축된다. DMZ의 소축척 평면도는 지구 표면에서 705 킬로미터(438 마일) 상공에 떠 있는 NASA/USGS Landsat 8과 같은 위성에서 생성된다.

두 번째 중간 스케일의 이미지는 언덕 꼭대기나 하늘을 나는 드론이 (120 미터/400 피트) 담은 DMZ의 모습이다.

마지막으로, 보다 근접한 스케일로 개인적인 경험들을 나타낸다. 이 사진은 내가 2011년 DMZ 현장을 답사하며 찍은 사진이다.

이 이미지들에서 보이는 세 가지 스케일은 DMZ의 다양한 특성을 묘사한다. 여러 거리에서, 다양한 기술을 통해 생산된 이미지들은 DMZ에 대한 여러 해석을 가능하게 한다.

또한 다양한 시각이 동일한 물체나 현상에 대해 여러 가지 의미와 이야기를 만들어 낼 수 있다는 사실을 지적하고 있다.

+ 120m (400 ft) Drone imagery

Perspective view - S / XS

+ 0.00 m (0 ft) Ground

Dongsei Kim © Oct 2022

Short-term >>

화쟁(和諍) 그리기

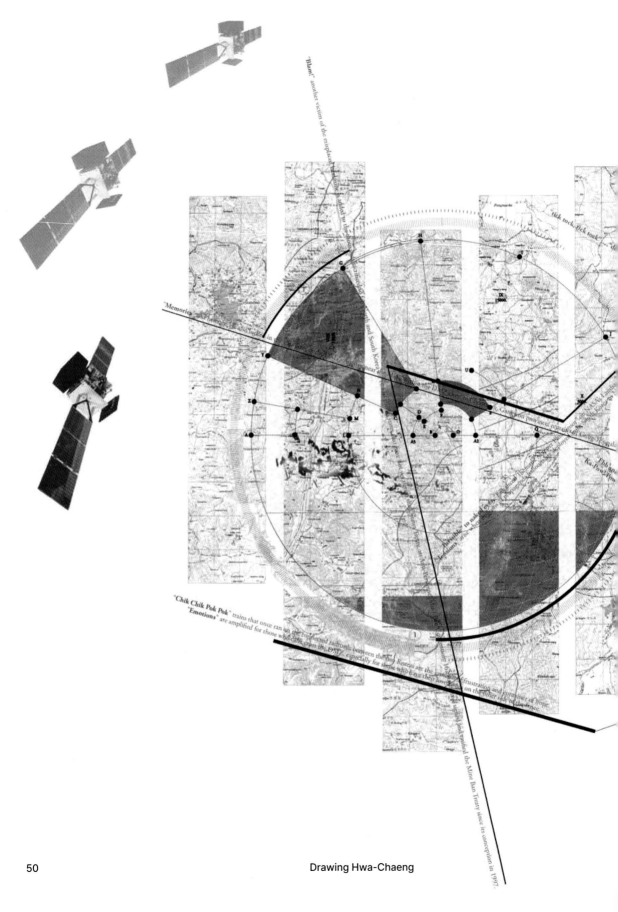

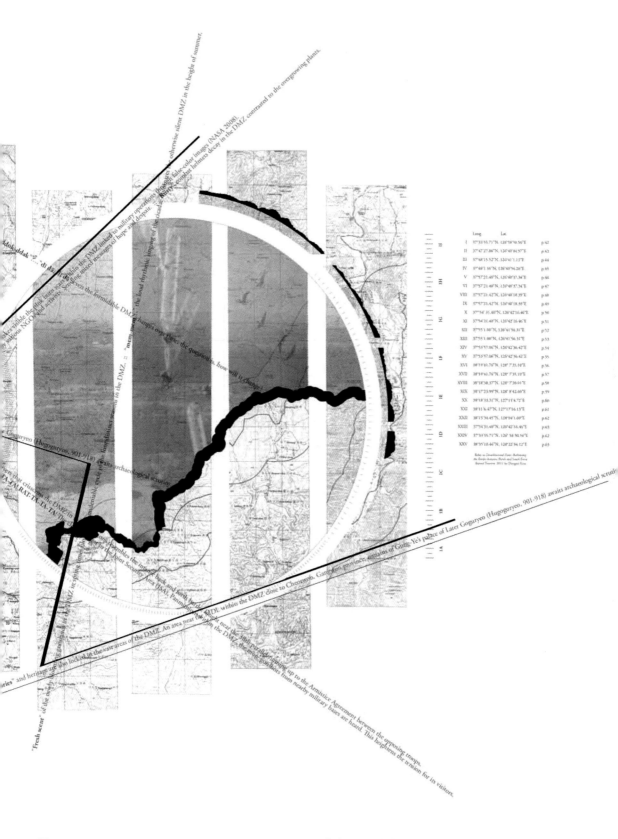

The Second Iteration: Uncovering the Agency of the Unknown Armistice Maps[1]

『Second Iteration: Uncovering the Agency of the Unknown Armistice Maps』 essentially deconstructs and reconstructs the underexposed armistice maps of the DMZ for novel interpretations.

By interrogating the relationship between the 'line drawn on a map' and the disjunctive spatial result produced over time, it helps us to rethink the habitual relationship between borders and their maps.

These maps further activate senses, emotions, memories, and human subjectivities that examine the impacts of borders on individual and collective human psyche.

Moreover, in doing so these ongoing mapping projects provoke a critical rethinking of nation-states and how border apparatuses operate to constantly sustain them.[2]

"두 번째 반복: 알려지지 않은 정전협정 지도의 힘/역할 발굴하기"는 본질적으로 잘 알려지지 않은 정전협정 지도들을 해체하고 재구성하여 새롭게 해석하는 작업이다.

'지도에 그려진 선'과 시간이 지남에 따라 생성된 공간들과의 괴리를 질문함으로써 국경과 국경을 나타내는 지도 특유의 관계를 재고해 본다.

이런 지도들은 감각, 감정, 기억, 그리고 인간의 주관성을 활성화하여, 국가의 경계가 개인과 집단의 심리에 어떤 영향을 미치는지를 살펴볼 기회를 제공한다.

이런 현재 진행형 매핑 프로젝트들은 민족국가와 그를 유지하는 도구인 국경이 어떻게 작동하는지에 대한 비판적인 재고를 불러일으킨다.[2]

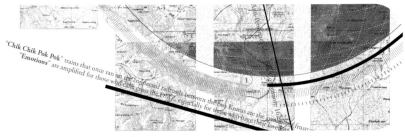

"Chik Chik Pok Pok" "Emotions" trains that once ran on the connected railroads between the two Koreas are amplified for those who can't cross the DMZ, especially for those who have their loved ... frustr...

1.
『The Second Iteration: Uncovering the Agency of the Unknown Armistice Maps』 in the 『(im)positions - multimodal negotiations of place-identity』 exhibition curated by Kelum Palipane at the Dulux Gallery, Melbourne School of Design, University of Melbourne. 2017.

2.
Kim, Dongsei. 2016. 『The First Iteration』, 『The Site Magazine』 35 (Spring): 28-37. In print and online (http://www.thesitemagazine.com/read/the-first-iteration) (ISSN 2369-9566)

3.
Corner, James. 1999. "The Agency of Mapping: Speculation, Critique and Invention." in 『Mappings』 Edited by Dennis Cosgrove. London: Reaktion Books. Page 239.

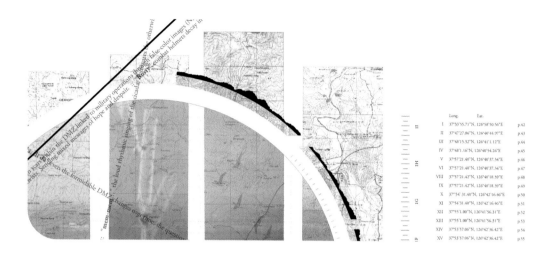

	Long.	Lat.	
I	37°53'55.71"N,	126°58'50.56"E	p.42
II	37°47'27.86"N,	126°40'44.97"E	p.43
III	37°48'15.52"N,	126°41'1.12"E	p.44
IV	37°48'1.16"N,	126°40'54.26"E	p.45
V	37°57'21.40"N,	126°40'37.54"E	p.46
VI	37°57'21.40"N,	126°40'37.54"E	p.47
VIII	37°57'21.42"N,	126°40'18.39"E	p.48
IX	37°57'21.42"N,	126°40'18.39"E	p.49
X	37°54'31.40"N,	126°42'16.46"E	p.50
XI	37°54'31.40"N,	126°42'16.46"E	p.51
XII	37°55'1.00"N,	126°41'56.31"E	p.52
XIII	37°55'1.00"N,	126°41'56.31"E	p.53
XIV	37°53'57.06"N,	126°42'36.42"E	p.54
XV	37°53'57.06"N,	126°42'36.42"E	p.55

"In other words, the unfolding agency of mapping is most effective when its capacity for description also sets the conditions for new eidetic and physical worlds to emerge"[3].

"다시 말해서, 매핑의 힘/역할은 새로운 직관적(直觀的)인 물리적 세계가 출현할 수 있는 조건을 설정할 때 가장 크게 발휘된다."[3]

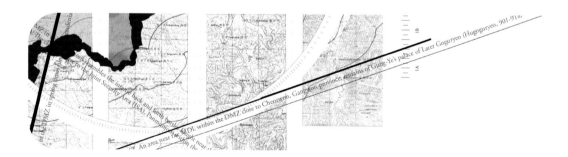

The Forgotten 533 Places and Names

This preliminary map sheds light on the forgotten 533 places within the Korean Demilitarized Zone (DMZ). The DMZ is a 250-km long and 4-km wide buffer zone that has been bisecting the Korean peninsula since the end of the Korean War in 1953. The names of the 533 places include 466 villages, 20 townships, 13 mountains, 12 rivers, and two cities marked within the boundaries of the Demilitarized Zone in the original 1953 Armistice Agreement map, a piece of document intended for the "the peaceful settlement of the Korean question" of all military forces involved at the time. No one would have imagined that the DMZ would still exist in 2022, some 69 years later.

Under the Armistice Agreement, "no person, military or civilian" is allowed to enter or cross the DMZ unless authorized. Since the official signing of the Agreement, the inhabitants of these 533 villages were forced to leave their homes and abandon their hometowns to go to either North or South Korea. These places within the DMZ have since been inaccessible, uninhabited, and mostly forgotten for the last 69 years. One of the main aims of this map is to better understand the impacts of political borders on human settlements, especially when access to a place is severely restricted for an extended period. Further, it attempts to highlight the history of the under-documented villages within the DMZ in contrast to the better-studied new strategic post-Korean War re-settlements near the border regions such as the Unification Villages, Tongilchon on the South Korean side.

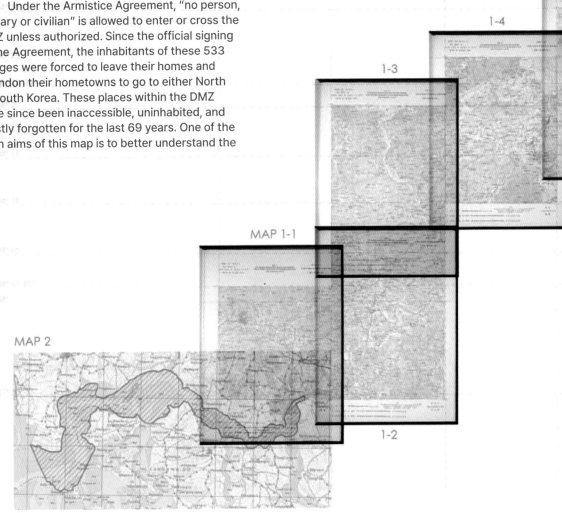

1-4

1-3

MAP 1-1

MAP 2

1-2

잃어버린 533개의 장소들과 지명들

The 533 names shown on this map were extracted, traced, categorized, and listed from the 1:50,000 scaled Armistice Agreement map. These forgotten names and places show how abstract lines on a map could extensively impact people's daily lives in zones of conflict. They also illustrate how arbitrarily drawn-up lines, i.e. territorial borders, have been inscribed into people's daily lives that cause long-term human suffering. In addition, the North Korean government has demarcated a "Special Military Region" drawn up to 50-km away

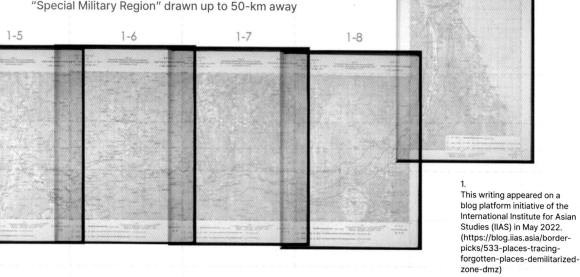

1.
This writing appeared on a blog platform initiative of the International Institute for Asian Studies (IIAS) in May 2022. (https://blog.iias.asia/border-picks/533-places-tracing-forgotten-places-demilitarized-zone-dmz)

from the DMZ, which has further prevented civilian access to the border regions. The South Korean side of border is equally highly restricted through the additional "Civilian Control Area" buffer zone that range between 15-20-km away from the Military Demarcation Line (MDL). These lines and zones exacerbate the historical amnesia as silent markers of separation.

Villages Chunggang-ni, Hongwon-ni, Unjong-ni listed on this map are some of the few 533 forgotten places extracted from the Armistice Map. These villages were populated before the Korean War. They were prosperous places close to Cheorwon, one of the largest transportation hubs on the Kyoungwon Main Line railway network and one of the top rice-producing regions. Nevertheless, it is challenging to find in-depth historical information on these places and what happened to their residents after the Korean War

due to long-term neglect and indifference towards these places.

This one-of-a-kind preliminary map of the forgotten 533 places acknowledges the history of the DMZ, emphasizing what existed and who lived there before the Armistice Agreement, eliciting emotions and memories of homes and homelands. This map challenges the dominant representations of the DMZ as a tabula rasa; instead, the mapping raises several questions: Who were the individuals that used to live in these places? How many were there? How and when did they leave? Where did they go? Are those who have lost their homes and hometowns still alive? Has the DMZ been taken over by flora and fauna over the years? How has nature transformed these places? What happens when the DMZ becomes accessible again? And when that happens, who would be entitled to claim ownership of what remains within the DMZ ?

THE FORGOTTEN 533

486 Villages (동,통,리,반...)   **12** Rivers (천, 강)

20 Townships (면)   **2** Cities (시)

13 Mountains (산)

CITIES (시)

문월시, [Munwolsi]
수욱시, [Suuksi]

TOWNSHIPS (면)

고성면, [Kosong-myon]
군내면, [Kunnae-myon]
궁북면, [Kunbung-myon]
근동면, [Kundong-myon]
금화면, [Kumhwa-myon]
남면, [Nam-myon]
묘장면, [Myojang-myon]
북면, [Buk-myun]
삭녕면, [Sangyong-myon]
상녕면, [Sangnyong-myon]
수동면, [Sudong-myon]
수입면, [Suim-myon]
왕징면, [Wangjingmyon]
원동면, [Wondong-myon]
인목면, [Inmong-myon]
임남면, [Imnam-myon]
장단면, [Changdan-myeon]
장도면, [Changdo-myon]
중면, [Chung-myon]
중면, [Chung-myon]

VILLAGES (동,통,리,반...)

가남동, [Kanam-dong]
가단리, [Kadan-ni]
가라치, [Karach'i]
가마골, [Kamagol]
가마굴, [Kama-gol]
가재동, [Kajae-dong]
가질리, [Kach'il-li]
가질평, [Kach'il-bong]
간건현, [Kanjmhyon]
간촌, [Kanch'on]
갈골, [Kal-gol]
갈동, [Kal-dong]
갈마, [Kalma-gogae]

갈현동, [Karhyon-dong]
갈현리, [Kalhyun-ri]
갈현리, [Karhyon-ni]
갈화골, [Karhwa-gol]
감봉리, [Kambong-ni]
감암동, [Kamam-dong]
감월리, [Kamwol-li]
감호, [Kam-ho]
감호, [Kam-ho]
강정, [Kangjong]
강정리, [Kangjong-ni]
거리실, [Korisil]
계당촌, [Kyedangchon]
계호동, [Kyehe-dong]
고걸동, [Kogwol-tong]
고령, [Korung]
고동곡, [Kodonggol]
고랑포리, [Korangpo-ri]
고랑포리, [Korangpo-ri]
고루리, [Koru-ri]
고미싱리, [Komisong-ni]
고양대, [Koyangdae]
고왕리, [Kowang-ni]
고작동, [Gojak-kol]
고산동, [Gojan-dong]
고잔상리, [Kojansang-ni]
고잔하리, [Kojanha-ri]
고잔하리새마을, [Kojanhari]
고장동, [Kojang-dong]
고장리, [Kojang-ni]
고지동, [Koji-dong]

고황봉, [Kohwang-bong]
곽촌, [Kwakchon]
관포동, [Kwanp'o-dong]
광대골, [Kwangdae-gol]
광대도, [Kwangdae-dong]
광명리, [Kwangmyong-ni]
광삼리, [Kwangsam-ni]
구골, [Ku-gol]
구골, [Ku-gol]
구룡동, [Kuryong-dong]
구만리, [Kuman-ni]
구봉촌, [Kubongch'on]
군돌, [Kundol]
군신동, [Kunsan-dong]
굴벗우, [Kulbyore]
굴전, [Kulchon]
궁마을, [Kungmal]
궁곡, [Kumgok]
굼곡리, [Kumgongni]
금곡리, [Kumgong-ni]
금룡리, [Kumnung-ni]
금송촌, [Kumsong-ch'on]
곰암동, [Kumam-dong]
금척동, [Kumch'ok-tong]
금촌, [Kimchon]
기공리, [Kigong-ni]
짚은골, [Kip'ungol]
나부골, [Nabu-gol]
낡은동, [Nalgun-dong]
낡은리, [Nalgunto'o]
남대촌, [Namedae-ch'on]

남전동, [Namch'on-dong]
내동, [Nae-dong]
내동, [Nae-dong]
내리, [Nae-ri]
내면리, [Naemyon-ni]
내봉촌, [Naebongch'on]
내성동리, [Naesongdong-ni]
내유, [Naeyu]
내촌, [Naech'on]
내풍동, [Naep'ung-dong]
내허평, [Naehop'yong]
내허평, [Naehop'yong]
냉정, [Naengjong]
냉정동, [Naengjong-dong]
노북골, [Nolbut-gol]
노동, [No-dong]
노동리, [Nodong-ni]
노하리, [Noha-ri]
노하리, [Noha-ri]
논고개, [Non-kogae]
논곡, [Non-gol]
농만마을, [Nunganmal]
뇌암, [Noeam]
누룸고개, [Nurum-kogae]
능동, [Nung-dong]
다락댁, [Taraktae]

38°22'30
38°20'

성자동, [Songja-dong]
송동, [Song-dong]
송산리, [Songsan-ni]
송산리, [Songsan-ni]
송어직, [Songojik]
송정, [Sohjong]
송촌동, [Songch'on-dong]
송현, [Songhyon]
송현리, [Songhyon-ni]
수고치, [Sugotchi]
수구네미, [Sulgu-nemi]
수동리, [Sudong-ni]
수령지, [Surongji]
수령, [Suryong]
수륜리, [Suryun-ni]
수오동, [Suo-dong]
숙고개, [Suk-hyon]
숭양리, [Sungyang-ni]
습학동, [Sunghak-tong]
시다막, [Sidamak]
신기, [Singi]
선대리, [Sindae-ni]
신란리, [Sint'an-ni]
신목동, [Simmok-tong]
진촌리, [Sinch'onni]
신현리, [Sinhyon-ni]
씽두동, [Ssangdu-dong]
아곡, [Agok]
아래후동, [Arashu-dong]
안터골, [Ant'ogol]
야초, [Yadch'on]
약산동, [Yaksan-dong]
약촌, [Yakch'on]
양곡, [Yangok]
양지, [Yangji]
양지마을, [Yangjimal]
양지촌, [Yangji-ch'on]
어룡개, [Oryongpo]
어룡리, [Oryong-ni]
어적신리, [Ojoksan-ni]
어항리, [Ohang-ni]
여곡, [Yo-gol]
여내골, [Yonaegol]
염대, [Yangdae]
오가덕, [Ogadok]
오금리, [Okum-ni]
오리동, [Ori-dong]

단령, [Tal-lyong]
당원리, [Tangwon-ni]
당촌, [Tangch'on]
당추촌, [Tanghach'on]
대강리, [Taegong-ni]
대경대, [Taegyong-]
대곡, [Taegok]
대궐대, [Taegwolt]
대마리, [Taema-ri]
대성동, [Taesong-]
대아재, [Taeyajae]
대위도, [Taewi-do]
대평, [Taep'yong]
덕마을, [Tangmal]
덕령, [Tongnu]
덕산리, [Toksan-n]
덕산리, [Toksan-n]
덕운골, [Togun-go]
덕잔리, [Toksan-n]
덕현골, [Tokhyon-]
도동, [To-dong]
도라산리, [Torasan]
도람, [Toryom]
도로산리, [Torasan]
도막동, [Tomak-to]
도미현, [Tomihyon]
도원리, [Homihni]
도연니, [Toyon-ni]

오리정, [Orijong]
오소동, [Oso-dong]
오룡리, [Oum-ni]
오장동, [Ojang-dong]
오촌, [Och'on]
외둔지, [Wadunji]
와전, [Wach'on]
외대봉, [Oedaebong]
외면리, [Oemyon-ni]
외면현, [Oemyan-hyan]
임성동리, [Oesongdong-]
외유, [Oeyu]
외풍동, [Oep'ung-dong]
용동, [Yong-dong]
우근리, [Ugun-ni]
운무란, [Unmurhan]
운정리, [Unjong-ni]
웃개막이, [Utkkaemugi]
웃후동, [Woothu-dong]
원당리, [Wondang-ri]
원대, [Wondae]
월두평, [Woltup'yong]
월정리, [Woichongni]
월정리, [Wolchong-ni]
유정리, [Yujong-ni]
율동, [Yul-tong]
율목동, [Yulmo-tong]
율목리, [Yulmong-ni]
움달마을, [Umdalmal]
운곡, [Ungok]
운곡, [Un-gol]
음지일, [Umn-ch'on]
이목동, [Imok-tong]
이실골, [Isil-gol]
일원동, [Irwan-dong]
일은동, [Irun-dong]
자개동, [Chagae-dong]
작목동, [Changmak-tong]
작학동, [Chakhak-tong]
잔과리, [Changwa-ri]
잣골, [Chat-kol]
장군골, [Changgun-gol]
장성동, [Changsong-don]
장승리, [Changsung-ni]
장지산동, [Changjisan-do]
장촌, [Changchon]
장파리, [Changpa-song]
장평동, [Changpyong-do]
강항, [Changhang]
적금리, [Chogum-ni]
적전리, [Chokchon-ni]

38°15'
38°10'
38°05'
38°01'30"
38°
127°15'10.4"
127°00'10.4"
126°45'10.4"

Fig. A

서후동, [Sahu-dong]
신곡동, [San'gok-tong]
산골, [San'gol]
산명리, [Sanmyong-ni]
산명호, [Sanmyong-ho]
산전, [Sanjon]
산점리, [Sanjom-ni]
산후동, [Sanhu-dong]
삼거리, [Samgo-ri]
삼막골, [Sammakkol]
삼복동, [Sambok-tong]
삼안골, [Saman-gol]
삼지령, [Sam'chi-ryong]
삼치령, [Samch'-i-ryong]
삼현, [Sam-hyon]
상가단골, [Sanggadan-gol]
상감령, [Sanggamnyang]
상고밀동, [Sanggomil-tong]
상덕리, [Sangdong-ni]

상목실, [Sangmoksil]
상쇠굼, [Sangsoegol]
상진리, [Sangjin-ni]
상산명동, [Sangjinmyong-dong]
새마을, [Saemal]
새말, [Saemal]
새말, [Saemal]
새별, [Sae-mal]
새터마을, [Saet'omal]
서궁리, [Sogong-ni]
서당골, [Sodang-gol]
서두물, [Sodumul]
서문리, [Soun-ni]
서장리, [Sojang-ni]
서희령, [Sohui-ryang]
서희리, [Sahui-ri]
석고개, [Sokkogae]
석사리, [Soksa-ri]
석장리, [Sokchang-ni]
선돌, [Sondol]
선벽, [Sonbyok]
선우목, [Sonumok]
성내동, [Songnae-dong]
상어월, [Songowol]
세현리, [Sohyon-ni]
소리, [So-ri]
소성동, [Sosong-dong]
소작봉, [Sojak-pong]
소학골, [Sohak-tong]
솔불, [Solmol]
송곡, [Songgok]
송곡리, [Songgong-ni]
송내동, [Songnae-dong]
송도진리, [Songdojin-ni]

도장골, [Tojang-dong]
도평리, [Top'yong-ni]
도피막, [Top'imak]
도화동, [Tohwa-dong]
도화동, [Tohwa-dong]
독거리, [Tokkom-ni]
독창동, [Tokchang-dong]
통강리, [Tonggang-ni]
동마골, [Tongmal]
동막, [Tongmak]
동모리, [Tongmori]
동장리, [Tongjang-ni]
동장원, [Tanghach'on]
동편촌, [Tongpyonchon]
두매리, [Tumae-ri]
두명동, [Tumyong-dong]
두속동, [Tusok-tong]
두포동, [Tup'o-dong]
등대리, [Tungdae-ri]
둥대리, [Tungdae-ri]
라부리, [Nabu-ri]
마가대, [Mah'gadae]
마군골, [Magun-gol]
마담리, [Madam-ni]
마대동, [Madae-tong]
마란동, [Maran-dong]
마명동, [Mamyong-dong]

마산곡, [Masangok]
마장리, [Majang-ni]
막대동, [Maktae-dong]
막애동, [Magae-dong]
만도, [Mando]
만석동, [Mansok-tong]
만언리, [Manyon-ni]
맘소, [Mangso]
매계, [Maegye]
매돌바우, [Maettolbau]
매현리, [Maehyon-ni]
명륜동, [Myongnyun-dong]
목실리, [Moksil-li]
옥관동, [Mokkwan-dong]
목욕골, [Megyok-kol]
무대, [Mudae]
문동리, [Mundung-ni]
미록동, [Mirok tong]
바다울, [Padaul]
바우골, [Pau-gol]
바우절골, [Paujol-gol]
박동, [Pak-tong]
방는동, [Pangnung-dong]
빅달, [Paktal]
빅달골, [Patt'ogol]
밤성골, [Pamsong-gol]

방내동, [Pangnae-dong]
방동, [Pang-dong]
방동, [Pang-dong]
방석동, [Pangsok-tong]
방어다리, [Pangodari]
방죽골, [Pangch'uk-tol]
빙죽동, [Pangch'uk-tong]
빙죽동, [Pangchuk-tong]
방터골, [Pangto-gol]
방통리, [Pangt'ong-ni]
배고개, [Paejae]
배선골, [Paeson-gol]
배암, [Paeam]
배둘, [Paettul]
백권리, [Paekkwon-ni]
백동물리, [Paektongum-ni]
백석동, [Paeksok-tong]
백월포, [Paegilp'o]
백진리, [Paekchon-ni]
백학동, [Paekhak-tong]
뱀골, [Paem-gol]
벌마을, [Polmal]
벌말, [Palmal]
범길, [Polmal]
별우, [Pyoru]
보광동, [Pogwang-dong]

복개, [Pokkae]
봉길리, [Ponggil-li]
봉당덕리, [Pongdangdong-ni]
봉미, [Pongmi]
봉수동, [Pongsu-dong]
부흥리, [Puhung-ni]
북정령, [Pukchong-nyang!]
북장, [Pukch'ang]
불당동, [Pultang-dong]
붕초원, [P'ungch'on-won]
뺄골, [Poael-gol]
사곡, [Sagok]
사교, [Sogyo]
사기막, [Sagimak]
사가점, [Segajom]
사내골, [Sanae-gol]
사동, [Sa-dong]
사래리, [Sat'ae-ri]
사비리, [Sabi-ri]
사임, [Saam]
사아사동, [Sayasi-dong]
사창동, [Sach'ang-dong]
서천리, [Sach'on-ni]

38°30'
38°25'
128°15'10.4'

127°45'10.4'
128°00'10.4'

적전리, [Chokchon-ni]
점마을, [Chommal]
점촌, [Chomchon]
정골, [Chong-gol]
정동리, [Chongdong-ni]
정자마을, [Chongjamal]
조산리, [Chosan-ni]
조항곡, [Chohanggol]
좌초, [Chwaso]
주토소, [Chut'oso]
주토소, [Chut'oso]
죽대리, [Chuktae-ri]
중강리, [Chunggang-ni]
충고잔, [Chunggojan]
충동, [Chung-dong]
충목실, [Chungmoksil]
중사리, [Chungsa-ni]
줄세리, [Chungse-ri]
충어성, [Chungosong]
지감라, [Chigam-ni]
지금리, [Chigum-ni]
지로동, [Chiro-song]
지룡동, [Chirung-dong]
지심동, [Chisang-dong]
지음동, [Chium-dong]
지촌, [Chich'on]
직동, [Chik-tong]
진곡리, [Chin'gong-ni]
진촌, [Chinch'on]
진촌, [Chinch'on]
진현리, [Chinhyon-ni]
찬골, [Chan'gol]
창골, [Ch'ang-gol]
창나리, [Ch'angnae-ri]
천당동, [Ch'ondang-dong]
절미동, [Ch'olmi-dong]
청소곡, [Chungsogok]
청용리, [Ch'ongnyong-ni]
청정리, [Ch'ongjong-ni]
청장리, [Chungjung-ni]
체금리, [Chegum-ni]
초구, [Ch'ogu]
초록동, [Chorok-tong]
추촌, [Ch'uch'on]
칠청동, [Ch'ilchong-dong]
칠청동, [Ch'ilchong-dong]
탄동, [T'an-dong]
탑골, [T'ap kol]
탑상동, [T'apsang-dong]
토기점, [T'ogijom]
토기전, [T'ogijom]

통골, [T'ong-gol]
통선골, [T'ongson'gol]
판문집, [Paomunjom]
판부동, [P'anbu-dong]
팔산리, [Palsan-ni]
평창동, [P'yongch'ang-dong]
평촌, [P'yongch'on]
포리, [P'o-ri]
포의진리, [P'ooejin-ni]
포촌리, [P'och'un-ni]
포춘동, [P'och'un-dong]
포남동, [Pyonam-dong]
풍곡, [P'unggok]
풍골, [P'ung-gol]
풍천원, [P'un'gch'on-won]
피루개, [P'irugae]
하김령, [Hagamnyong]
하개막이, [Hagaemagi]
하고밀동, [Hagamil-tong]
하덕리, [Hadong-ni]
하독검도, [Hadokkom-gol]
하동, [Ha-dong]
하두촌, [Haduch'on]
하물한, [Hamurhan]
하삭곡, [Hasakkol]
하우개, [Haugae]
하진리, [Hajin-ni]
하진명도, [Hajinmyong-dong]
하진현, [Hajinhyon]
하탄리, [Hat'an-ni]
하토동, [Hat'o-dong]
히푱동, [Hap'ung-dong]
학당리, [Haktang-ni]
한탄촌, [Hant'an-ch'on]
항골, [Hanggol]
항동리, [Hangdong-ni]
해산대, [Haesamdae]
험석동, [Homsok-tong]
형제현, [Hyongje-hyon]
호당리, [Homangni]
횽원리, [Hongwon-ni]
화소척, [Hwasoho]
화전동, [Hwajon-dong]
황기, [Hwanggi]
황명동, [Hwangnyong-dong]
회산동, [Hoesan-dong]
회우, [Hoeu]
후동, [Hu-dong]
후동리, [Hudong-ni]
후천동, [Huchon-dong]
흑석동, [Huksok-tong]

MOUNTAINS (산)

계룡산, [Kyeung-san]
고왕산, [Kowang-san]
마량산, [Maryang-san]
백악산, [Paekhak-san]
상가산, [Sanggasan]
상마산, [Sangmasan]
석팡산, [Sokkpangsan]
성재산, [Songjae-san]
약산, [Yaksan]
조산, [Chosan]

중가산, [Chunggasan]
중마산, [Chungmasan]
하가산, [Hagasan]

RIVERS (천, 강)

금성천, [Kumgong-ch'on]
금성천, [Kumsong-chen]
남강, [Nam-gang]
사미천, [Samich'on]
사미천, [Sami-ch'on]
사천, [Sa-ch'on]
삼류천, [Sangryu-ch'on]
서천, [So-ch'on]
석천, [Sokchon]
수입천, [Suip-ch'on]
역곡천, [Yokkok-ch'on]
후천, [Huch'on]

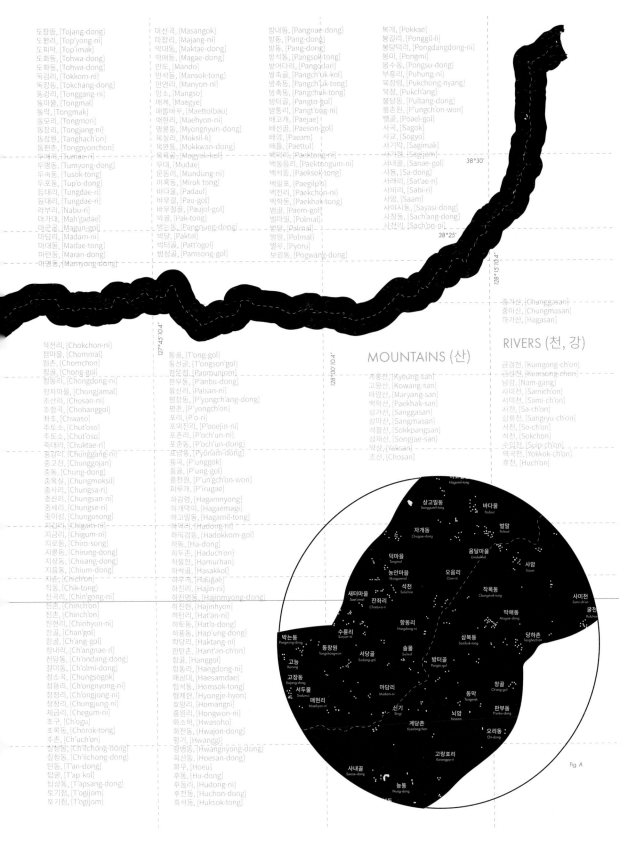

Fig. A

화쟁(和諍) 그리기

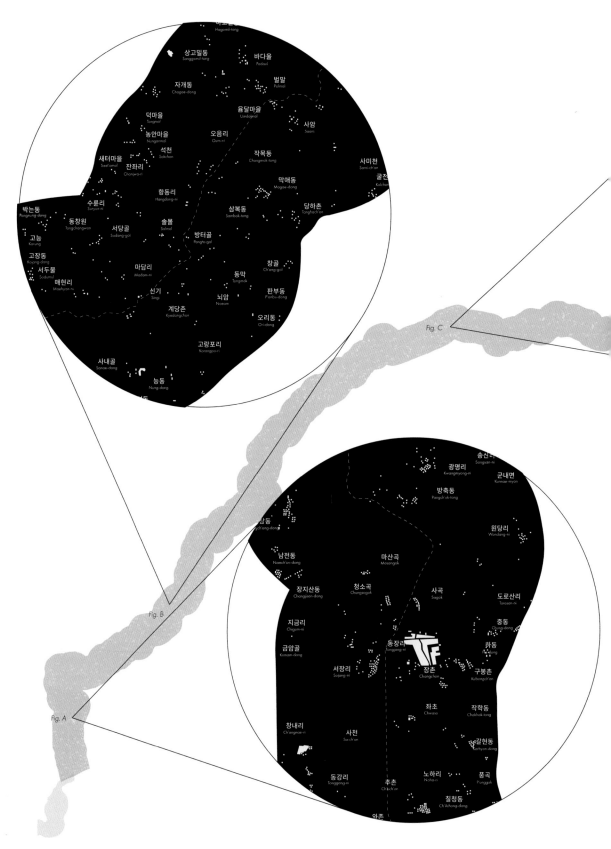

Fig. A

Fig. B

Fig. C

Drawing Hwa-Chaeng

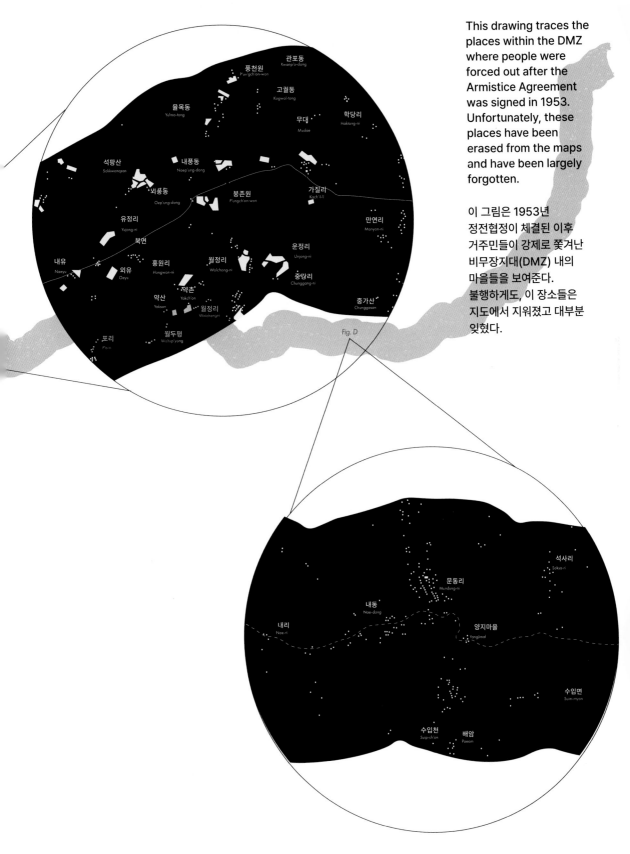

This drawing traces the places within the DMZ where people were forced out after the Armistice Agreement was signed in 1953. Unfortunately, these places have been erased from the maps and have been largely forgotten.

이 그림은 1953년 정전협정이 체결된 이후 거주민들이 강제로 쫓겨난 비무장지대(DMZ) 내의 마을들을 보여준다. 불행하게도, 이 장소들은 지도에서 지워졌고 대부분 잊혔다.

Fig. D

화쟁(和諍) 그리기

Productive Generation(s) Redux

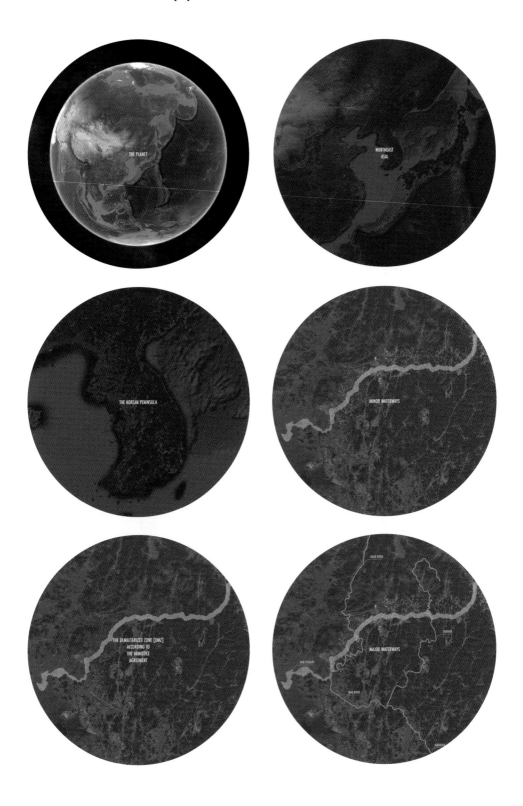

Drawing Hwa-Chaeng

생산적인 세대/발전의 귀환

1.
I designed 『Generation(s)』 project in 2002, twenty years ago in 『Narrative Design』 course instructed by Daniel Brown, when I was a undergraduate student at Victoria University of Wellington in New Zealand. 『Generation(s): A Productive Landscape in the DMZ』 revisits this architectural manifestion of the DMZ with my more recent mapping research.

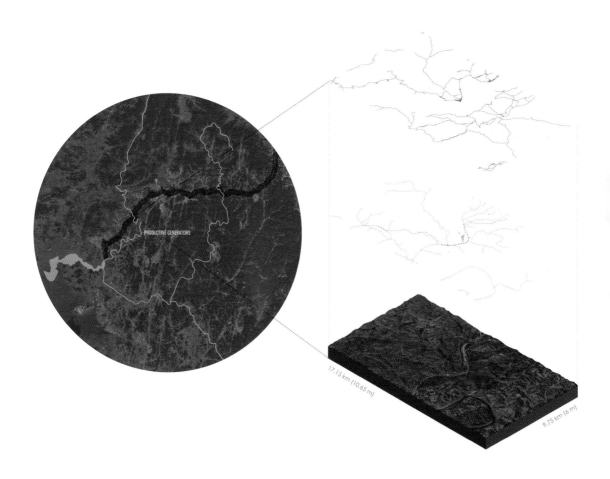

PRODUCTIVE GENERATORS

17.15 km (10.65 m)

9.75 km (6 m)

This experimental project retroactively builds on a student project I designed 20 years ago.[1] The retroactive mapping (pages 60-65) post rationalizes a naive student design project from the past. This kind of mapping adds diversely scaled meaningful stories to architecture. Further, it explores and expands the role of architectural intervention for an impossible site.

이 실험적 매핑은 20년 전 나의 학생 프로젝트를 소급하여 창작한 것으로,[1] 천진한 디자인 프로젝트를 합리화한다 (60-65쪽). 이러한 매핑은 건축에 다양하고 의미 있는 이야기들을 여러 스케일로 더한다. 또한 비무장지대에 대한 건축적 개입의 역할과 가능성을 탐색하고 확장한다.

화쟁(和諍) 그리기

Generating Fertile Grounds for ⋯
Echinophora
Hanabusaya

Generating Power + Memories
Memorial for the lost generations - deceased separated families
Micro hydro plant generating electricity for both Koreas

Generating New Polity with Water
Bridge of no return
Joint Security Area (JSA)
Panmunjom

Han River Estuary

Generating Ecological Infrastructure for Fau ⋯
Red-Crown crane
Black-faced spoonbill

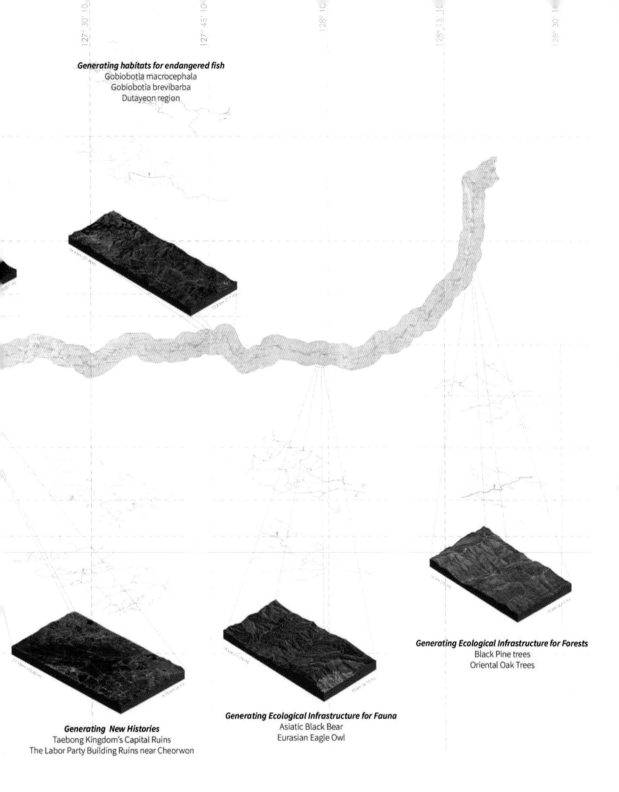

Generating habitats for endangered fish
Gobiobotia macrocephala
Gobiobotia brevibarba
Dutayeon region

Generating Ecological Infrastructure for Forests
Black Pine trees
Oriental Oak Trees

Generating Ecological Infrastructure for Fauna
Asiatic Black Bear
Eurasian Eagle Owl

Generating New Histories
Taebong Kingdom's Capital Ruins
The Labor Party Building Ruins near Cheorwon

화쟁(和諍) 그리기

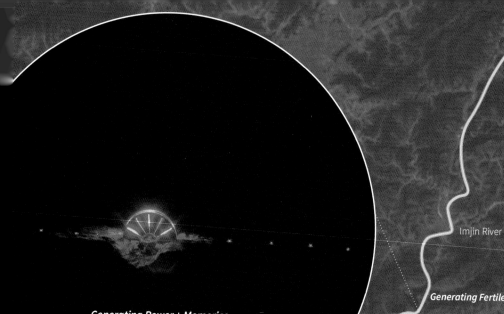

Generating Power + Memories
Memorial for the lost generations - deceased separated families
Micro hydro plant generating electricity for both Koreas

38°08'55.0"N
126°58'00.2"E

Imjin River

Generating Fertile Grounds for Flora
Echinophora
Hanabusaya 38°17'46.6
127°06'44.

Generating Ecological Infrastructure for Fauna
Red-Crown crane
Black-faced spoonbill 38°02'23.8"N
126°51'21.5"E

Generating New Polity with Water
Bridge of no return
Joint Security Area (JSA)
Panmunjom 37°57'22.0"N
126°40'12.8"E

Generating Estuarial Economy & Ecology
Joint survey projects
Migratory bird watching
Fishing Industries

Han River Estuary

Han F

Imnam Dam

Generating Ecological Infrastructure for Forests
Black Pine trees
Oriental Oak Trees

Generating New Histories
Taebong Kingdom's Capital Ruins
The Labor Party Building Ruins near Cheorwon

38°19'57.4"N
127°14'03.4"E

Generating habitats for endangered fish
Gobiobotia macrocephala
Gobiobotia brevibarba
Dutayeon region
38°19'18.4"N
127°47'53.1"E

Generating Ecological Infrastructure for F
Asiatic Black Bear
Eurasian Eagle Owl

38°19'11.1"N
127°59'09.0"E

The Demilitarized Zone (DMZ)

Peace Dam

Bukhan River

Generation(s): A Productive Landscape in the DMZ[1]

The Demilitarized Zone (DMZ) has bisected the Korean Peninsula into North and South Korea since 1953. The DMZ is a resultant of the Korean War, considered a proxy war between the "Free World" and the "Communist bloc." This 250-km long and 4-km wide border zone operates as a symbol of the ongoing Cold War, which performs as an impenetrable border between the two Koreas.

The Generation(s) project reimagines this typically contested territory as a productive landscape by acknowledging its past and illustrating its alternative futures. Further, it demonstrates how it can become a landscape for experimentation for the inter-Korean relationship.

First, the Generation(s) project traces the waterways that flow through the human-made border. The act of tracing the water emphasizes large-scale natural elements against the human-made political construct. Generation(s) project identifies eight significant points along the DMZ where the waterways and the center of the DMZ (Military Demarcation Line (MDL)) meet and proposes design interventions that generate different kinds of productive futures for the contested border.

These intersections are developed as part of the whole into productive landscapes that engage the sites history, ecology, economy, flora, fauna, and geology. One of the intersections are transformed into a site of power generation and a place to remember the lost generations of the separated families.

화쟁(和諍) 그리기

Building Ojakkyo: Reimagining DMZ's next 69 years[1]

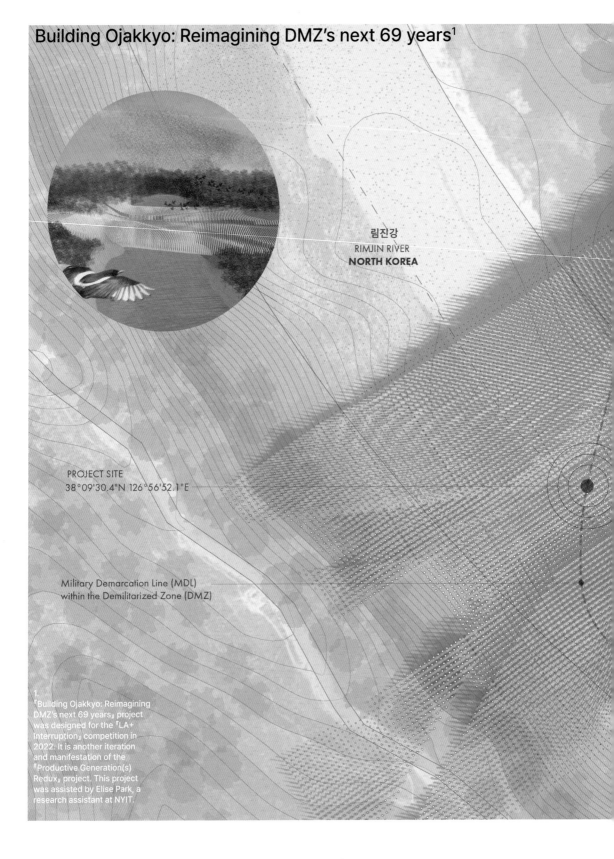

림진강
RIMJIN RIVER
NORTH KOREA

PROJECT SITE
38°09'30.4"N 126°56'52.1"E

Military Demarcation Line (MDL)
within the Demilitarized Zone (DMZ)

1.
『Building Ojakkyo: Reimagining
DMZ's next 69 years』 project
was designed for the 『LA+
Interruption』 competition in
2022. It is another iteration
and manifestation of the
『Productive Generation(s)
Redux』 project. This project
was assisted by Elise Park, a
research assistant at NYIT.

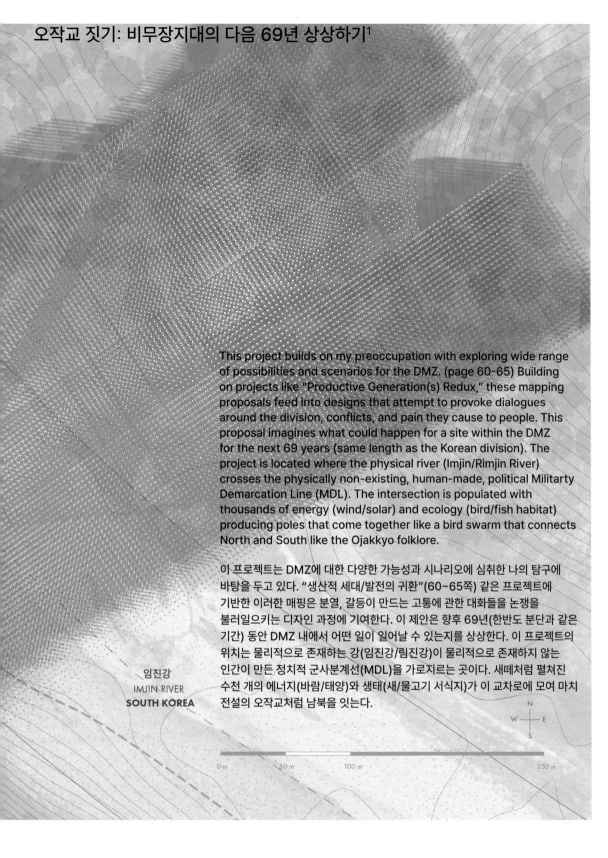

오작교 짓기: 비무장지대의 다음 69년 상상하기[1]

This project builds on my preoccupation with exploring wide range of possibilities and scenarios for the DMZ. (page 60-65) Building on projects like "Productive Generation(s) Redux," these mapping proposals feed into designs that attempt to provoke dialogues around the division, conflicts, and pain they cause to people. This proposal imagines what could happen for a site within the DMZ for the next 69 years (same length as the Korean division). The project is located where the physical river (Imjin/Rimjin River) crosses the physically non-existing, human-made, political Militarty Demarcation Line (MDL). The intersection is populated with thousands of energy (wind/solar) and ecology (bird/fish habitat) producing poles that come together like a bird swarm that connects North and South like the Ojakkyo folklore.

이 프로젝트는 DMZ에 대한 다양한 가능성과 시나리오에 심취한 나의 탐구에 바탕을 두고 있다. "생산적 세대/발전의 귀환"(60~65쪽) 같은 프로젝트에 기반한 이러한 매핑은 분열, 갈등이 만드는 고통에 관한 대화들을 논쟁을 불러일으키는 디자인 과정에 기여한다. 이 제안은 향후 69년(한반도 분단과 같은 기간) 동안 DMZ 내에서 어떤 일이 일어날 수 있는지를 상상한다. 이 프로젝트의 위치는 물리적으로 존재하는 강(임진강/림진강)이 물리적으로 존재하지 않는 인간이 만든 정치적 군사분계선(MDL)을 가로지르는 곳이다. 새떼처럼 펼쳐진 수천 개의 에너지(바람/태양)와 생태(새/물고기 서식지)가 이 교차로에 모여 마치 전설의 오작교처럼 남북을 잇는다.

임진강
IMJIN RIVER
SOUTH KOREA

N
W · E
S

0 m   50 m   100 m   250 m

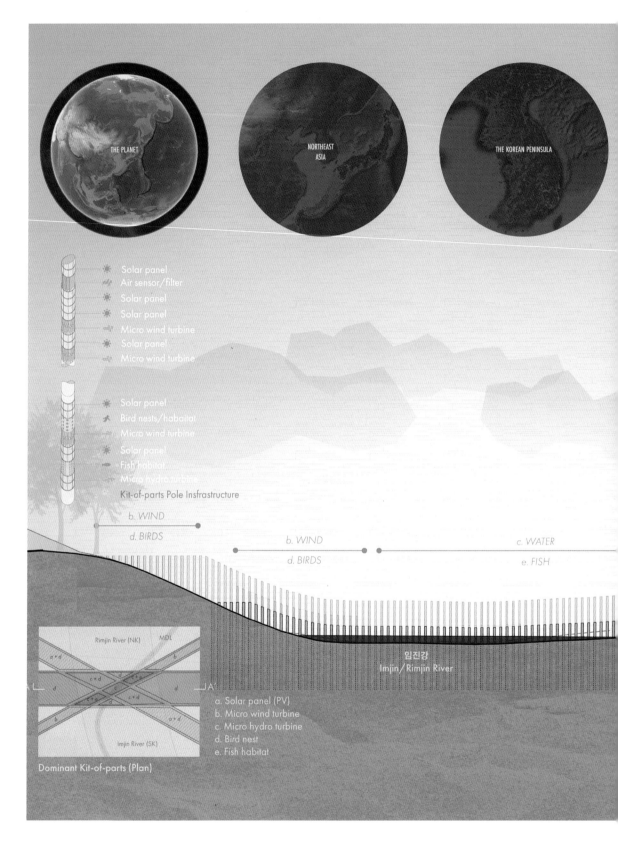

THE PLANET

NORTHEAST ASIA

THE KOREAN PENINSULA

Solar panel
Air sensor/filter
Solar panel
Solar panel
Micro wind turbine
Solar panel
Micro wind turbine

Solar panel
Bird nests/habaitat
Micro wind turbine
Solar panel
Fish habitat
Micro hydro turbine
Kit-of-parts Pole Insfrastructure

b. WIND
d. BIRDS

b. WIND
d. BIRDS

c. WATER
e. FISH

임진강
Imjin/Rimjin River

Rimjin River (NK)   MDL

a + d

b

d

c + d

d

A⌐   ¬A'

b

a + d

Imjin River (SK)

a. Solar panel (PV)
b. Micro wind turbine
c. Micro hydro turbine
d. Bird nest
e. Fish habitat

Dominant Kit-of-parts (Plan)

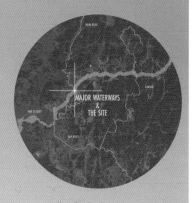

The Demilitarized Zone (DMZ) bisects the Korean Peninsula. This 4-km-wide and 250-km-long military buffer zone has effectively divided the Koreans since the end of the Korean War (1950~1953). This "interruption" project reflects on the DMZ's past 69 years and questions its potential to transform the current conflict into a positive and productive force for the next 69 years.

Societies battle to eliminate their perceived adversaries. Nevertheless, I believe opponents and frictions can be transformed into productive power when framed in a novel way, just as the friction from rubbing our hands gives us the desired warmth on a frigid day.

The "interruption" sits within the DMZ. More precisely, it is located where the DMZ's Military Demarcation Line (MDL) and the Imjin (how South Koreans say and write it)/Rimjin (how North Koreans say and write it) River intersect. This is where the human-made political line is interrupted by the ecological flows of nature. This project intensifies natural flows to question the absurd ideological lines.

The "interruption" is inspired by Chilseok Festival—originally a Chinese folklore (Qixi Festival) adopted by Koreans—where the crows and magpies come together once a year on lunisolar July the 7th to form a bridge (Ojakkyo) to reunite separated couple Altair (cowherd) and Vega (weaver girl) across the Milky Way. Japanese celebrate this day as Tanabata Festival and the Vietnamese as Thất Tịch Festival. Rain on this day is said to be the couple's tears.

"Ojakkyo" is a vertical kit-of-parts pole infrastructure and a grave marker built over time. The project starts with 89,188 poles that symbolize the number of deceased separated family members. One additional pole will be erected each time one of the remaining 44,449 separated families passes away. Where the Imjin/Rimjin River and the MDL meet, the poles interrupt the river flows with a series of micro-hydro turbines to produce electricity for both Koreas. Underwater areas also become fish habitats. Poles on hilltops and valleys become micro wind turbines. Poles with greater exposure to the sun are clad with PV panels. Other areas of the poles become nesting areas for birds.

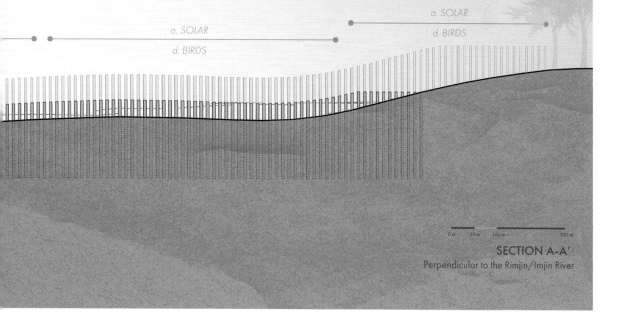

a. SOLAR

d. BIRDS

a. SOLAR

d. BIRDS

0 m   50 m   100 m   250 m

SECTION A-A'
Perpendicular to the Rimjin/Imjin River

화쟁(和諍) 그리기

The viewers of this exhibition were offered a physical and mental space where they could critically engage border discourses. The space consisted of mappings, photographs, collages, installations, texts, moving images with sounds, and interactive QR (Quick Response) codes. The multi-media exhibition aimed to bring about a spatial experience that illustrates how a conflicted border zone can be used to "project" future alternative scenarios through architectural analysis and research.

『Projecting the DMZ』exhibition, at Center Gallery, Education Hall, New York Institute of Technology. Photo credit: Dongsei Kim, 2019.

wing Hwa-Chaeng

이 전시는 국경 담론에 비판적으로 참여할 수 있는 신체적, 정신적 공간을
관람객들에게 제공했다. 이 전시 공간은 매핑, 사진, 콜라주, 설치, 텍스트,
소리가 있는 동영상, 상호 교환적 QR(Quick Response) 코드로
구성됐다. 이 멀티미디어 전시회는 충돌하는 국경지대가 건축 분석과
연구를 통해 미래 대안 시나리오를 '투영(投影)/기획/예상' 하는 데 어떻게
활용될 수 있는지를 보여주는 공간적 경험을 이끌어 내는 것을 목표로 했다.

화해(和諍) 그리기

Drawing Hwa-Chaeng

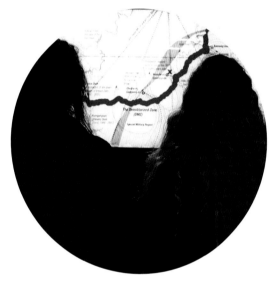

『Projecting the DMZ』 exhibition, at Center Gallery, Education Hall, New York Institute of Technology. Photo credit: Roger Yu, 2019.

화쟁(和諍) 그리기

Exhibition: Undoing the DMZ

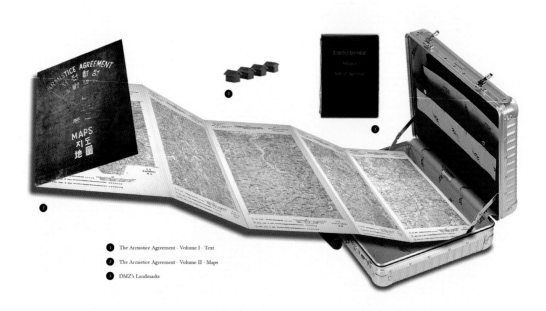

① The Armistice Agreement · Volume I · Text

② The Armistice Agreement · Volume II · Maps

③ DMZ's Landmarks

This is a playful work-in-progress portmanteau. It contains raw ingredients and instruments that allow Demilitarized Zone's stakeholders to explore its latent productive potential.

The portmanteau consists of three parts. The first part includes the reduced replica of the 1953 "Armistice Agreement Volume I-Text" written in three languages and the nine "Armistice Agreement Volume II-Maps." The second part includes several of my studies on the DMZ. The last part contains the architect's sketching instruments suggesting the designer's facilitating role in the future transformations of the DMZ. It also signifies a particular capacity of "architectural intelligence" to project DMZ's future through visual and experiential means.

These three parts together elucidate how the two Koreas constructed the DMZ, how we can interpret it, and how we can reenvision it through "architectural intelligence."

이 여행 가방은 유쾌하게 진행되고 있는 작업이다. 가방 안에는 비무장지대의 이해당사자들이 비무장지대에 잠재된 생산적 가능성을 탐구할 수 있는 재료와 도구들이 들어 있다.

가방을 채우는 세 가지는 첫 번째, 3개 언어로 작성된 1953년 "정전협정 제1권-협정문"과 9개의 "정전협정 제2권-지도" 축소 사본이다. 두 번째는 비무장지대에 대한 나의 연구들이다. 마지막은 미래 비무장지대의 변혁에서 디자이너로서 촉진적 역할을 제안하는 건축가의 스케치 도구들이다. 시각적이고도 경험적인, 세 가지 접근/방법이 의미하는 바는 비무장지대의 미래를 그려내는 '건축적 지성' 의 특별한 능력이다.

이 작업은 남북이 비무장지대를 어떻게 건설했는지, 우리가 어떻게 해석할 수 있는지, 그리고 '건축적 지성'을 통해 어떻게 새롭게 상상할 수 있는지를 설명한다.

전시: 비무장지대 풀어내기

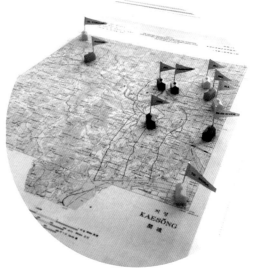

"Undoing the Demilitarized Zone (DMZ): The Agency of Architectural Intelligence" in 『ACSA Portmanteau Designs: Play with the Rules』 exhibition. Schroeder Galleria, Milwaukee Art Museum (MAM), Milwaukee, WI, USA. 2018. Curated by Jasmine Benyamin, Nikole Bouchard, Whitney Moon, Kyle Reynolds, and Mo Zell.[1]

1.
See more details in "Undoing the Demilitarized Zone (DMZ): The Agency of Architectural Intelligence" in 『Play with the Rules ACSA Fall Conference Proceeding』 Edited by Jasmine Benyamin, Kyle Reynolds, Mo Zell, Nikole Bouchard & Whitney Moon, 446-451. Washington, DC: ACSA Press. (ISBN 978-1-944214-28-9). (https://www.acsa-arch. org/chapter/undoing-the-demilitarized-zone-dmzthe-agency-of-architectural-intelligence/)

Generation(s), 2002.

생산적인 세대(世代)/발전(發電), 2002.

In October 2020, a few months after COVID-19 hit the globe, Dongwoo Yim of PRAUD (Progressive Research, Architecture, Urbanism, and Design), whom I have known for many years, invited me to initiate a "Pamphlet Architecture"- like publication with Yunhee Choi and Jinhong Jeon at BARE (Bureau of Architecture, Research & Environment) that would investigate the expanded role of architects beyond designing buildings. So, the conversation started. We met diligently every fortnight via Zoom, more than 40 times, for the last 20 months and this publication is a small part of that archive.

This publication allowed me to examine my past mapping projects within the context of my larger creative practice. Further, my constant conversations, back and forth, and feedback sessions between my Tiki-Taka colleagues— Dongwoo Yim, Jinhong Jeon, Yunhee Choi, and E Roon Kang—enriched my understanding of my own work from a different perspective. These constant dialogues were another way of understanding how my practice performs the notion of Hwa-Chaeng.

Selected mapping projects of my creative practice illustrate how they generate meaningful questions and how they transform differences, contradictions, tensions, and conflicts into ingredients for imagining alternative futures. This critical reflective process also illustrates a wide range of potential embedded in tools and methods of the architectural discipline for mapping.

I also explored how these approaches can produce meaningful mapping projects that generate questions and valuable knowledge for others. Making this publication also allowed me to use the book as a medium and its making process to present, refine, and organize my scattered thoughts. Some of the limitations of mapping that I was aware of, such as its dark past, as an effective tool for imperialism, colonization, and proliferation of late capitalism, became at times more apparent, which made me more acutely aware of the role of mapping.

My first thanks go to the publisher, jeongye-c-publishers, and their patience with my work. I would like to also thank Dean Maria Perbellini at NYIT, Lukas Pauer at University of Toronto, and my research assistants at NYIT: Peter Thompson, Julia Andor, and Elise Park, who assisted me throughout the production of this publication. My last thanks go to my extended family, especially my wife Yisoo and son Theo Seojin who inspire and support my intellectual pursuits.

코로나 바이러스가 전 세계를 강타한 지 몇 달 뒤인 2020년 10월, 여러 해 알고 지내던 PRAUD(Progressive Research, Architecture, Urbanism, and Design)의 임동우가 BARE(Bureau of Architecture, Research & Environment)의 최윤희, 전진홍과 함께《팸플릿 아키텍처》와 같은 출판물 작업을 통해 건축가의 역할을 건물 설계 그 이상으로 확대하는 것에 대한 연구를 제안했다. 그렇게 우리의 대화가 시작되었고, 지난 20개월 동안 한 달에 두 번씩 줌을 통해 만났고, 이 출판물은 약 40회에 걸친 대화 기록의 일부이다.

나는 이 출판물을 통해 나의 매핑 프로젝트들을 연구와 실무라는 큰 맥락 속에서 살펴볼 수 있었다. 나아가 티키타카 동료 임동우, 전진홍, 최윤희, 강이룬, 강정예 편집장과 지속적인 대화와 오가는 피드백 속에서 나의 작업을 또 다른 관점에서 이해하게 되었다. 이러한 끊임없는 대화는 나의 작업들이 어떻게 화쟁의 개념을 수행하는지를 이해하는 또 하나의 방법이었다.

이 책에 소개된 매핑 프로젝트들은 어떻게 의미 있는 질문들을 생산하는지, 그리고 그것들이 어떻게 다름, 모순, 긴장, 갈등을 대안적인 미래를 상상하는 요소로 변화시키는지를 보여준다. 이 비판적이고 사색적인 프로세스는 건축 분야의 도구와 방법에 내재된 광범위한 잠재력이 어떻게 매핑에 사용될 수 있는지도 보여준다.

또한 나는 다양한 질문들과 사람들에게 가치 있는 지식을 창출해 내는 데 의미 있는 매핑 프로젝트를, 어떻게 이러한 접근 방식이 만들어 낼 수 있는지 탐구했다. 이 출판물 또한, 책을 매개체로 삼아 흩어진 나의 생각을 다듬고 정리하여 보여줄 수 있게 해 주었다. 제국주의, 식민지화, 후기 자본주의의 확산에 효과적인 도구로서 이바지했던 어두운 과거와 같이, 내가 이미 알고 있던 매핑의 일부 한계가 때때로 더욱 뚜렷해졌고, 이는 나로 하여금 매핑의 역할을 더욱 예리하게 인식하게 했다.

우선 정예씨 출판사의 인내심에 감사를 표한다. 또한 NYIT의 건축 및 디자인 학과 학장 마리아 페르벨리니, 토론토 대학의 루카스 파우어, 그리고 이 출판물을 제작하는 동안 나를 도와준 NYIT의 연구 조교 피터 톰슨, 줄리아 안도, 그리고 엘리스 박에게 감사의 마음을 전한다. 나의 가족, 특히 나의 지적 추구에 영감을 주고 지지해 주는 이수 씨와 서진에게 마지막 감사를 보낸다.

Selected Resources & References

Kim, Dongsei. 2022. "533 Places: Tracing the Forgotten Places in the Demilitarized Zone (DMZ)" in "The Blog of International Institute for Asian Studies (IIAS)" (https://blog.iias.asia/border-picks/533-places-tracing-forgotten-places-demilitarized-zone-dmz).

Kim, Dongsei. 2021. "Towards a Dynamic Mapping: Deconstructing Borders" in "Reading Beyond" edited by Bert De Jonghe & Fatma Mhmood (Harvard University Graduate School of Design) April 2021. pp. 106-109. (ISBN:987-1-7340480-5-6).

Kim, Dongsei. 2021. "Projecting the DMZ." New York, NY: Blurb. (ISBN: 978-1-00-606859-1)

Kim, Dongsei. 2021. "Workshop: Imagining the Impossible: The DMZ" In "Beyond Table: An Archive of Future School Summer Studio: Transborder Lab," curated by Hae-won Shin Art Council Korea, May 2021. pp 121-131.

Kim, Dongsei. 2021. "Future School: The Korean Pavilion 17th International Architecture Exhibition La Biennale Di Venezia catalogue," curated by Haewon Shin Art Council Korea, 2021. pp. 24, 25, 46. (ISBN: 987-0-9915263-1).

Kim, Dongsei. 2020. "Demilitarized Zone's Interstitial Villages" Red Envelope 02: In-between. No. 02 (September) 10-13.

Kim, Dongsei. 2020. "Borders as Urbanism: A Preliminary Study on Realigning Border Rivers as Productive Spaces." The Journal of Seoul Studies Vol. 79 (Summer): 61-69. (DOI: 10.17647/jss.2020.05.79.61. ISSN:1225-746X).

Kim, Dongsei. 2019. "How the architecture of border walls creates division (or inspires trust)" "Salon." March 2.

Kim, Dongsei. 2019. "A Construct The Koreas (Never) Made Together Deconstructing the DMZ For The Imaginary-2019." (English version). https://www.youtube.com/watch?v=YlRk8L1Xpr0

Kim, Dongsei. 2019. "남북한이 함께 만든 (만들지 않은) 구축물: 상상을 위한 비무장지대의 해체-2019" (Korean version). https://www.youtube.com/watch?v=E2FWQ0Yqj7M

Kim, Dongsei. 2018. "Metamorphosis of a Zone." "Topos." 104: 74-79. September.

Kim, Dongsei. 2018. "Undoing the Demilitarized Zone (DMZ): The Agency of Architectural Intelligence." In "Play with the Rules ACSA Fall Conference Proceeding." Edited by Jasmine Benyamin, Kyle Reynolds, Mo Zell, Nikole Bouchard & Whitney Moon, 446-451. Washington, DC: ACSA Press. (ISBN 978-1-944214-28-9)

Kim, Dongsei. 2018. "Mapping Precedes Territory: Forays into Representations of the Air Defence Identification Zones (ADIZs) in East Asia." Transect Journal 2 (April): 20-33. Chicago Design Office. April.

Kim, Dongsei. 2017. "Towards Edge Spaces of Productive Inclusivity: A Subversive Act." In "Chandigarh Rethink: Transforming Ruralities & Edge(ness) in Global Urbanities," edited by Manu P. Sobti, 92-105. Chambersburg, PA: ORO Editions.

Kim, Dongsei. 2016. "The First Iteration." "The Site Magazine." Vol. 35. Spring. May 26: 28-37. (ISSN 2369-9566)

Kim, Dongsei. 2014. "A Construct the Koreas (Never) Made Together: Deconstructing the DMZ for the Imaginary" & "Lines of War." In "Crow's Eye View: The Korean Peninsula" edited by Hyungmin Pai and Minsuk Cho, 192-194 & 195-197. Seoul: Archilife. (ISBN 978-89-964508-6-3 93610)

Kim, Dongsei. 2014. "A Construct The Koreas (Never) Made Together Deconstructing the DMZ For The Imaginary." https://vimeo.com/93697167

Kim, Dongsei. 2014. "Towards a Dialogical Peace in the Demilitarized Zone." "Volume." Vol. 40. July: 40-43. (ISSN 978-90-77966)

Kim, Dongsei. 2014. "Imagining the Impossible: Reflecting on Moments in Flux." "Inflection: Journal of the Melbourne School of Design" 1 (November): 112-114. (ISBN 978-3-88778-427-0)

Kim, Dongsei. 2014. "A White Paper on the Demilitarized Zone: Some Facts and Questions for the Future." & "A Construct the Koreas (Never) Made Together: Deconstructing the DMZ for the imaginary." In "The North Korea Atlas," edited by Dongwoo Yim & Rafael Luna, 105-111 & 566-571. Seoul: DAMDI Publishers.

Kim, Dongsei. 2013. "The Demilitarized Zone: Redrawing the 151-mile Border between North and South Korea." In "101st Proceedings-New Constellations New Ecologies," edited by Ila Berman and Ed Mitchell, 518-528. Washington, DC: ACSA Press. (ISBN: 978-0-935502-84-8)

Kim, Dongsei. 2013. "Borders as Urbanism: Redrawing the Demilitarized Zone (DMZ) between Democratic People's Republic of Korea and Republic of Korea." "Landscape Architecture Frontiers." Vol.1 (2) April: 150-157.

Kim, Dongsei. 2012. "Border as Urbanism: Redrawing the Demilitarized Zone (DMZ) between North and South Korea." Master in Design Studies; Research Thesis. Harvard University, Graduate School of Design, Cambridge, MA.

Kim, Dongsei. 2011. "Demilitarized Zone: Redrawing the Border between North and South Korea Beyond Tourism." Cambridge, MA: Blurb.

Dongsei Kim is as an Assistant Professor of Architecture at the New York Institute of Technology and founded axu studio in 2010. His research on the Korean Demilitarized Zone was invited to the Golden Lion Award-winning Korean Pavilion at the 14th Venice Architecture Biennale. He has published in journals such as "Topos," "Volume," "Inflection," "Landscape Architecture Frontiers," and in books such as the "Crow's Eye View" and "The North Korean Atlas". He has taught at Columbia University, Carleton University, Korea University, and RMIT. He received his MDesS (Dist) from Harvard University, MSAUD from Columbia University, and a B.Arch (Hons) from Victoria University of Wellington. He first registered as an architect with the New Zealand Registration Board (NZRAB) in 2007 and is an Architect member of the New Zealand Institute of Architecture (ANZIA).

김동세는 뉴욕 공과대학 건축학과에서 조교수로 재직하고 있으며 axu studio를 2010년에 설립했다. 그의 한반도 비무장지대 관련 작업은 2014년 황금사자상을 수상한 제 14회 베니스 건축 비엔날레 한국관 전시에 초청받았다. 그의 연구는 〈Topos〉와 〈Volume〉, 〈Inflection〉, 〈Landscape Architecture Frontiers〉 등의 저널과 《Crow's Eye View》, 《The North Korean Atlas》 등의 서적을 통해 출간되었다. 컬럼비아대학교, 칼턴대학교, 고려대학교, RMIT에서 강의했으며 하버드대학교에서 디자인학 석사, 컬럼비아대학교에서 도시와 건축디자인 석사, 웰링턴 빅토리아대학교에서 건축학사 학위를 받았다. 뉴질랜드 건축사를 2007년에 취득하였고 뉴질랜드 건축가 협회 정회원이다.

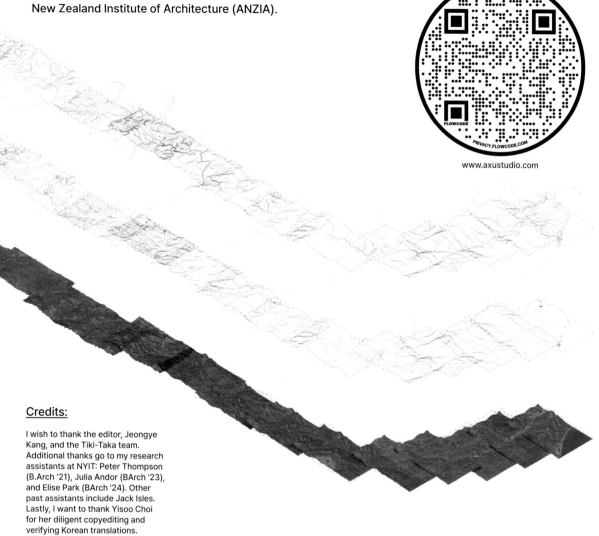

www.axustudio.com

Credits:

I wish to thank the editor, Jeongye Kang, and the Tiki-Taka team. Additional thanks go to my research assistants at NYIT: Peter Thompson (B.Arch '21), Julia Andor (BArch '23), and Elise Park (BArch '24). Other past assistants include Jack Isles. Lastly, I want to thank Yisoo Choi for her diligent copyediting and verifying Korean translations.

Our thinking

Most often, the practice of architecture is limited as to making buildings. However, architects tell their unique stories in multiple ways. They write, curate exhibitions, and conduct a wide range of research; moreover, architects also design and make new products. We can consider all of these activities as architectural acts.

Tiki-taka focuses on architects' diverse methods and processes beyond the making of buildings. It further focuses on engaging the public through exploring architects' thinking, projects, and processes, beyond critiquing architecture. Moreover, Tiki-taka aims to produce and expand architectural discussions by collaborating and interacting with a wide range of disciplines.

— Tiki-taka experiments with new and diverse architectural discourses
— Tiki-taka seeks to generate multi-directional conversations
— Tiki-taka explores new architectural discussions through open dialogues
— Tiki-taka recognizes architecture beyond building architecture and creates new architectural narratives
— Tiki-taka endeavours to produce and expand architectural discussions and collaborate with a wide range of disciplines
— Tiki-taka aspires to expand the diverse architectural thinking with a learning mindset

Written by E Roon Kang, Dongsei Kim, Dongwoo Yim, Jeongye Kang, Jinhong Jeon, Yunhee Choi

Drawing Hwa-Chaeng :
Mapping Contested Territories for Imagination
by Dongsei Kim

우리의 생각

흔히 '건물을 짓는다'라는 제한된 의미로 건축을 정의하곤 하지만, 사실 건축가들은 다양한 방식으로 독자적인 이야기를 짓는다. 글을 쓰기도 하고, 전시를 기획하기도 하며, 다양한 리서치를 수행하기도 한다. 그리고 새로운 제품을 디자인하기도, 또 만들어 내기도 한다. 이 모든 것을 건축가들이 하는 건축 행위라 볼 수 있다.

티키타카는 건물을 짓는 행위를 넘어 건축가들이 다양한 방식으로 이야기를 만들어 나아가는 과정에 주목한다. 건축 작품이나 그에 대한 비평이 아닌, 건축가들의 생각, 작업, 과정 등을 경쾌한 방식으로 다루며 대중과 소통하고자 한다. 나아가 건축의 외연을 확장하고 담론을 생성하며, 다양한 분야와의 협업과 소통을 열어갈 것이다.

— 티키타카는 새롭고 다양한 건축담론 플랫폼을 실험한다
— 티키타카는 일방향이 아닌 다방향의 대화를 생성한다
— 티키타카는 책장 안에 갇힌 이론이 아닌 열린 소통을 통한 건축담론을 실험한다
— 티키타카는 건축이 건물 설계 이상의 행위임을 인식하고 새로운 건축의 이야기를 만들어 나간다
— 티키타카는 건축의 외연을 확장하고 다양한 분야와의 협력을 모색한다
— 티키타카는 배우는 자세로 다양한 건축사고의 확장을 모색한다

강이룬, 강정예, 김동세, 임동우, 전진홍, 최윤희 씀

화쟁(和諍) 그리기: 상상을 위한 분쟁지역 매핑

지은이 김동세
초판 1쇄 발행일 2022년 12월 28일

펴낸이 강정예 펴낸곳 정예씨 출판사
프레임워크 강이룬 서체 지원 프리텐다드(길형진)
제작 영림인쇄

ISBN 979-11-86058-33-6
ISBN 979-11-86058-26-8 (SET)

HOW DO _YOU_ DEFINE ARCHITECTURE?
HOW IS THIS EVOLVING FOR YOU?

HOW CAN ARCHITECTURAL
METHODS CONTRIBUTE TO
THINGS OTHER THAN
BUILDING BUILDINGS?

WHAT DOES DIVERSITY MEAN IN
ARCHITECTURE?

HOW DO YOU COLLABORATE WITH OTHERS?

WHAT PROCESS IS COMMON BETWEEN
WRITING A BOOK & BUILDING
ARCHITECTURE?

IS ARCHITECTURE KNOWLEDGE?

HOW DOES RESEARCH INFORM
YOUR PRACTICE?

WHAT IS A CONSTANT INSPIRATION
THAT INFORMS YOUR RESEARCH
& PRACTICE?

WHAT WORKED? WHAT FAILED?
WHY? WHAT DID YOU LEARN?

WHAT NEXT?
WHAT IS YOUR PREOCCUPATION?